THE KITCHEN TABLE
ENTREPRENEUR

THE KITCHEN TABLE ENTREPRENEUR

AN

INSPIRATIONAL

GUIDE TO

TURNING YOUR

HOBBY INTO

A PROFITABLE

BUSINESS

PAUL POWER

howtobooks

Published by How To Books Ltd
3 Newtec Place, Magdalen Road
Oxford OX4 1RE, United Kingdom
Tel: (01865) 793806 Fax: (01865) 248780
email: info@howtobooks.co.uk
www.howtobooks.co.uk

British Library Cataloguing in Publication Data.
A catalogue record for this book is available from the British Library.

Cover design by Baseline Arts Ltd, Oxford
Produced for How To Books by Deer Park Productions, Tavistock
Typeset by PDQ Typesetting, Newcastle-under-Lyme, Staffs.
Printed and bound by Bell & Bain Ltd, Glasgow

NOTE: The material contained in this book is set out in good faith for general
guidance and no liability can be accepted for loss or expense incurred as a result of
relying in particular circumstances on statements made in the book. Laws and
regulations are complex and liable to change, and readers should check the current
position with the relevant authorities before making personal arrangements.

Contents

Preface

I started my first business when I was thirteen years of age. Then acting on well-meaning advice, I went to college, got a real job and became thoroughly miserable until finally later in life I rediscovered the excitement, fun and freedom that can only come with starting your own business.

I believe that if all you have right now is a hobby or an interest then you have enough to start your own business.

My aim in writing this book is to introduce you to the possibilities that are already within your reach and once you identify those that appeal to you most to give you a framework from which to start. I'll also be sharing with you the benefit of my experience in starting and running a business.

I invite you to join me in a life-changing experience by turning your hobby into a successful business.

If you would like to share your experiences, hopes fears and desires for the future visit my website at www.paulpower.co.uk

Good Luck and best wishes

Paul Power

Dedication

This book is dedicated in fond memory of Douglas Wright. A man whose entrepreneurial spirit was overshadowed only by his enormous generosity, kindness and willingness to help others fulfil their dreams.

Acknowledgements

My thanks to:

Giles and Nikki at How To Books for their support and encouragement with this project.

Melanie Jarman for her valuable contributions and help in the final preparations of the manuscript and for restoring my faith in boot fairs!

To Brian my partner and fellow KTE for his unfailing patience in putting up with daft ideas while quietly pointing our businesses in the right direction.

Finally thank you to all our customers, past, present and future – we hope that you've enjoyed our innovative approach as much as we have serving you.

1

How to Turn Any Hobby into a Business

WHAT IS KITCHEN TABLE ENTREPRENEURSHIP?

Put simply, it's where you find something you really enjoy doing and then look for ways of turning your hobby into a successful, profitable business without any huge financial risk or investment on your part.

Let's say, for example, that you're a keen walker and enjoy spending all of your spare time exploring and walking. You now want to run your own business doing something around your favourite hobby.

There are lots of potential opportunities. The ones that immediately spring to mind are:

◆ selling walking gear
◆ organising walking holidays
◆ writing and selling walking guides
◆ starting a pet-sitting service
◆ a gardening maintenance company
◆ a playschool
◆ a language school

- running your own hire business renting out anything from bouncy castles to boats
- starting and running your own holiday company: walking holidays, sailing holidays, history holidays...
- organising tours: garden tours, history tours, mystery tours...
- arranging dinner dates for single people
- offering your services as a home-sitter, pet-sitter, chaperone service....

Whatever your hobby or interest there is no end to the types of businesses you can start. The possibilities are endless. Who knows where this journey will take you? One thing's for sure, it will never end. That's the wonderful thing about running your own business. You'll never stop learning new things. You'll never wake up in the morning with that awful feeling that your life is dictated by someone else. Because, starting today, you're taking control of your life. Starting right now you're going your own way.

When I embarked on this same journey some years ago I was filled with excitement, which was overshadowed by worry. I'm delighted to say that some years on I'm still as excited as I was when I first started out. The only thing that I've lost is the worry factor. For I've learnt that worry is the most unproductive emotion that you can have. When you decide to take control of your own future, you lose that worry for you alone are responsible for your future.

I've also come to accept that on this road you never stop learning. Neither is there a right or a wrong way. Provided you have determination, passion and motivation there really is no such thing as failure. Although it's quite likely the business you start out with will not be the same business you end up with!

My first dip into the water of self-employment was a catering business, which died on its feet shortly after it began. The experience didn't deter me, but made me more determined to succeed. My next business was a gardening business, which is still with me today. Along the way I've been instrumental in starting a cycling business, a boat hire business, a gardening school as well as having a hand in lots of other areas. That's the great thing about being a KTE (Kitchen Table Entrepreneur). You can get involved in lots of different things. If something doesn't work, learn from it and move on. That's the secret. Move on. Only fools dwell on mistakes and failures. Successful people simply pick themselves up and start again.

The concept

OK. So let's look a bit more the concept of Kitchen Table Entrepreneurship. Let's imagine that you're a keen walker and have decided that you're going to sell walking gear.

As a keen walker you're in an excellent position to know what gear's worth buying and what to avoid. So you could set up your own mail order business, either working from a website and/or advertising in magazines read by walkers.

Where Kitchen Table Entrepreneurship differs is that rather than rush out and open a traditional walking/outdoor shop you instead run your business from home. The reason I suggest the kitchen table is that if you're like I was and don't have the luxury of having a spare room available, let alone any spare space in your home, you can run the administration side of your business from somewhere at home, and then hire some form of relatively inexpensive storage for your merchandise.

The advantages to this are:

◆ low overheads – no shop or office rents, insurances etc
◆ the advantages that come from working from home
◆ you can run your business around your life as opposed to running your life around your business.

At the same time, you could organise walking holidays. You could run this business either separately or alongside selling your walking gear. Again, rather than sign up to an expensive, tedious shop lease agreement, you could open an online business where not only could you sell walking gear but also walking holidays.

The enormous benefit of having a website as opposed to a high street shop is that you have access to a worldwide customer base, something you won't get with a traditional high street business.

Of course you could have a high street business and a website, but is it worth all that additional expenditure? And what about the hours? To survive and succeed your shop will need to be open seven days a week and are you really ready to commit yourself to standing behind the counter for long hours, or having to hire in costly staff to do it for you?

The smart alternative is to take the KTE route and work the business around your lifestyle, keeping overheads low and profits high.

WHAT MAKES KITCHEN TABLE ENTREPRENEURS DIFFERENT?

Kitchen Table Entrepreneurs make the best of what they have in terms of their personal skills. This and their financial resources means they start their businesses from where they are standing right now.

Rather than moan about what they could achieve if only they had enough money, the right premises or the right people, KTEs start their businesses with however much or little they have at the time.

Therefore if their ultimate aim is to have a trendy high street florists, but they can only afford a plastic bucket, they start with the bucket and work up. Lots of successful businesses have started this way.

The five personal strategies that every KTE lives by:

1. Start your business around something you love.
2. Develop self-motivation and reliance.
3. Look for the opportunity in everything.
4. Set written goals.
5. Never take rejection personally.

START YOUR BUSINESS AROUND SOMETHING YOU LOVE

The reason you participate in a particular hobby is that it makes you happy. It's a way of escaping from the daily grind of work, bosses, commuting and all that you don't like about your life. Imagine for a moment that you could spend the rest of your life working at something you really enjoy, and earning your living from it. How happy would you be? Successful people are happy people. Not because they are simply happy making money, but they are happy doing what they do. Money and financial rewards should always take second place to the primary goal of working at something you really enjoy doing.

DEVELOP SELF-MOTIVATION AND RELIANCE

One of the first things you'll find when you start your own business is that you will have to motivate yourself.

When I look back at those times in my life when I was most unhappy it was because I was living my life on others' terms. To succeed, I constantly needed others' support and encouragement. When this wasn't always forthcoming, I felt dejected and unhappy. The only way you can successfully start your own business is if you have developed unshakable self-reliance. No matter what comes at you, you know you will survive because you believe in yourself. You no longer need or seek others' approval. You know you can do it, and you don't need to turn to others for approval and motivation.

The greatest thing about being self-motivated is that you are the only person who can demotivate yourself.

◆ From now on, stop worrying about what others think of you.

◆ Stop caring about whether or not other people think you have what it takes to start your own business.

◆ Start looking inwardly for your strength and encouragement and soon your self-confidence will soar.

It is so important to learn the techniques of self-motivation. I say learn, because I believe our culture and conditioning doesn't always encourage us to rely on self-motivation. Rather than rely on motivating ourselves to do anything, many of us leave it to our teachers, employers, governments, partners, wives, husbands and so on. Sadly we never really learn how to ignite that spark within ourselves – the spark that at its best will spur us on to greatness, or if nothing else create the energy and enthusiasm to wake up every morning eager to try again.

Developing self-motivation is like learning anything new. It won't happen overnight and it takes practice, perseverance and time before you start reaping the rewards. But once you do you'll soon be able to exceed beyond your wildest dreams.

Working on your self-motivation

Start by suspending any cynicism. Work consciously at this. As soon as you hear that negative voice in your head, banish it from your mind.

The important thing here is to slam the door shut on that creeping paralysis called doubt. Usually when doubt creeps into your plans, its cousin, fear, is not far behind. They form a lethal combination and the only real way of overcoming them is to be completely self-motivated.

The three most powerful things you can do right now to develop your self-motivation are:

1. Visualise your success

The most powerful thing you can do to get started on the road to success is to start seeing yourself as successful. If you're ambition is ultimately to have a chain of high street stores or online retail outlets selling quality walking gear – then start seeing those shops. Visualise everything from the colour of the walls to how many staff you see working in your stores. From now on start working on your dream. The faster you can visualise your success, the more real and achievable your dreams become.

2. Start looking for possibilities

Successful entrepreneurs are different from other people in that they are always on the lookout for possibilities.

◆ EXPERIENCE ◆

After visiting Holland I decided I wanted to buy a Dutch bike as I believed nothing compared to these bikes in terms of comfort, quality and reliability. However when I tried to find somewhere in the UK to buy them, I couldn't. Rather than moan about the problem of trying to find a genuine Dutch bike in the UK, my business partner and I investigated the possibility of setting up our own shop specialising not only in Dutch bikes, but also in hard-to-find bikes. The sort of products that the multi-retailers wouldn't stock. Thus the Littlehampton Dutch Bike Company was born.

3. Start planning your goals

If your goal is to have a multi-chain of outdoor shops, start your goal planning with this as your principle and guiding goal.

Helping to visualise your success

This applies to everything, regardless of how insignificant the thing might be. Anything from getting a parking space to building a successful global empire will be achieved far more easily if you visualise a successful outcome from the start.

Don't believe me? Try this exercise.

Pick something you do regularly and find an absolute nightmare. Then before you do whatever this thing is again start visualising a successful outcome.

Let's say that usually when you go shopping in your car you find it absolutely impossible to find a parking space. But this time, before you even get into your car, start seeing that empty car parking space.

◆ Visualise it.
◆ See yourself effortlessly finding it.

◆ Experience the wave of relief wash over you as you drive into that space – your space.

When I was first told about this technique, I thought it was a load of nonsense. I mean, how could it be possible to conjure up a car parking space just by thinking positively about it? To my amazement it worked. The first time I tried this it worked. I couldn't believe how easy it was to find that space.

There's nothing magical about it. The fact is that we achieve what we expect to get. So if we set out with an entrenched negative view about something, usually we'll have a bad experience and 'prove' ourselves right.

However, when you start visualising success, all sorts of positive changes come about. Instead of looking for all the reasons why we should be unhappy, we concentrate on all the possibilities and our subconscious begins to work in actively seeking out ways of achieving what we want.

◆ TIP ◆

The bottom line is – You are what you think! Think negatively, and you'll be a negative person. On the other hand, start visualising successful outcomes in everything you do and you'll start seeing powerful, positive change in your life.

If you try this and it doesn't work first time then don't give up. It may take time and you must be prepared to suspend and resist your inbuilt cynicism.

Using this powerful technique in your business

Obviously the reason you're reading this book is that you want to turn your hobby into a business. But that's not all you're after. What you want is not simply to turn your hobby into a business, but also the benefits that come with it. For example:

◆ Enjoying the freedom of being your own boss.

- Earning a useful second income to pay for a holiday you wouldn't normally be able to afford.

- Building a successful, full-time business where others work for you while you enjoy the prestige and satisfaction that comes from owning a successful business.

Grab a piece of paper and a pencil and write down all the benefits you hope to achieve from starting your own business.

Include everything. If you hate working for your current employer and can't wait never to have to set foot in their premises again then include this. Write down how you'll feel when you walk out of the door for the last time. Write your leaving speech and a list of all those you'll invite to your leaving party.

When you've completed your lists, create a picture board.

Pictures are powerful motivators. So if one of your benefits is having a nice holiday every year, then go out and get the brochure of your dream holiday, cut out some pictures and paste them into your notebook. Or if your ultimate aim is to swap your current home for something more salubrious, get the details of your dream home from the estate agents and paste a picture into your notebook.

Don't forget the little benefits.

For example, if you're used to long, expensive, tedious commutes to work and your new business means you can work from home then include a copy of your over-priced rail ticket in your picture board and imagine what you can do with the money you save.

LOOK FOR THE OPPORTUNITY IN EVERYTHING

Successful people look for possibilities where others see only obstacles.

Many of the most successful Internet businesses have been born because their creators had a problem.

◆ **EXPERIENCE** ◆

Ebay was born because of a problem. The wife of its creator was a Pez collector. Remember those sweets that came in Pez's? Well her problem was that she couldn't find others who shared her hobby. Her husband came up with the solution – a collector's website – and from this innocuous beginning came what is now the world's largest online marketplace.

Whatever your hobby, I am sure there are things about it that will frustrate you. Perhaps you believe you're paying too much for something? Can't get it quick enough? Or whatever is available is unsuitable for the job you want to use it for?

Whatever the problem, welcome it. Grab it as a potential opportunity. Commit yourself that from now on you won't moan about it until you find the true opportunity that it presents.

Work at this technique and it'll pay dividends.

Start looking for possibilities

This means exploring every area of your hobby and finding opportunities, which means getting away from traditional thinking and really going deep! Going below the surface and what preconceptions you may have and really looking for those opportunities that exist everywhere.

Unfortunately when you mention the words 'hobby' and 'business' together most people think along traditional lines – for example a stamp collector selling stamps or an antiquarian book enthusiast trading books.

While undoubtedly these are real businesses opportunities, they are the obvious ones. Often it's the less obvious opportunities that offer the greatest potential.

◆ **EXPERIENCE** ◆

When the speed boat ride business ceased trading in our seaside town the ticket kiosk they had used fell into disrepair and became a target for vandals. Every time I walked along the seafront I became more despondent about how our beautiful area was being destroyed by anti-social behaviour. The solution was for one of our businesses to take it over, repaint it and bring it back to its original splendour. The kiosk became a home for our cycle hire business.

SETTING WRITTEN GOALS

Some years ago an experiment was carried out in the USA.

A group of students were asked to set their goals, which they all did with enthusiasm. Then some years later the researchers met again with the group to see how many had achieved their goals.

Disappointingly, most had not achieved anywhere near what they had wanted to. Only 3 per cent had achieved their goals. Those who had achieved, and in many cases exceeded, their initial expectations, were the ones who had made written goals.

The only certain way to achieve your goals is to have a written goal plan.

There are five steps to successful goal planning.

Step 1. Decide exactly what you want to achieve.
Instead of writing down something like, 'earning enough to go on an exotic holiday every year', describe it in detail. Record as much detail as you can about the holiday you want to go on and how much it's going to cost.

Similarly, if your goal in starting your business is to enjoy the freedom of working for yourself and building a secure and prosperous future for you and your family, then write it down in detail.

Allow yourself plenty of time to do this exercise. Your objective is to create tangible goals and not just vague statements.

Step 2. Set specific deadlines.

It doesn't matter how far in the future this is, but like the goal itself it must be detailed and specific.

Let's say your goal is to have your business up and running in three months from now. Get out your diary and work out the day your business will open for trade. Now commit yourself to this date by writing it in your diary, and on a calendar, and on a piece of paper that you keep with you at all times. Something like:

> 'On Monday, 10th March 2008, Jane's Walking Holidays opens for business.'

Step 3. Make a list.

Make a list of everything you will have to do to achieve your goals.

The best way to do this is, in no order whatsoever, think of everything you will need to do. List everything that comes into your head without thinking too much about it.

When you've finished, re-write your list into a logical sequence.

Then identify and prioritise the five most important things you need to do to achieve your goal.

Step 4. Start by working on the number one thing on your list.

Take action immediately on the number one most important thing you have highlighted on your list. Even if this is something as small as making a telephone call to enquire about getting further information on something, do it now.

While all the previous steps are essential to you achieving your goals, undertaking this step and the step that follows are crucial to your future success.

Step 5. Do something every day towards achieving your goals.
Work through your list and experience the enormous satisfaction of knocking things off your list.

◆ **TIP** ◆

Your success depends on keeping momentum going. This can easily be achieved so long as you do something, anything every day until you reach your goal.

You can use this technique for every area of your life and not just your business goals. It's a particularly useful way of getting yourself to focus on what's important in your life.

Don't forget it's vital to do something every day towards achieving your goals. Even if it's only to review your to-do lists, do it. Your success depends on you maintaining momentum and visualising the positive end results that you'll soon be enjoying.

NEVER TAKE REJECTION PERSONALLY

Successful salespeople never take rejection personally.

Accept that there will be times in the future when your ideas or your products will be rejected. Some people will laugh at what you're planning to do while others will offer well-meaning, but unhelpful, advice. Banks will refuse your loan applications and there are times when it will seem that everyone is against you.

The successful KTE takes this in their stride because they don't take things personally. You'll need to develop what I call 'politician shoulders' and steam ahead.

What I want you to do now is to grab a piece of paper or card, something small enough to fit into your wallet or purse, and write down the five strategies. Then from today on, get into the habit of reading these first thing in the morning and at various times throughout the day and start making a conscious effort to make them yours.

THE KTE PHILOSOPHY: FUN, FREEDOM AND PROFIT

These are the bedrock of any successful KTE business.

Fun

Starting and running your own business will require enormous commitment, hard work and dedication on your part. You'll probably have to learn new skills and do many things you've never done before, but believe me it's all worth it in the end. However, the road that lies ahead to your getting to that 'end' can be difficult and at times might seem impossible. That's why having fun is so important. Fun is one of those essential ingredients that's often overlooked when people start businesses. Therefore whatever business you're planning to start, make sure it revolves around doing something you really enjoy. Get this part right and the hard work is not only enjoyable but gives an enormous sense of self-achievement and well-being that you will never get while working for someone else.

Freedom

Having spent much of my earlier career working for an employer, I really do believe that nothing comes even close to the freedom of running your own business.

In a very short time from now you will be chief executive in your own business empire. It doesn't matter how small your operation is – what matters is that you are in charge of your future and the futures of those who mean so much to you.

And the greatest thing about working for yourself is that no one can make you redundant.

Profit

I recently sat in on a business start-up workshop full of hopeful would-be entrepreneurs. Everyone was full of enthusiasm for their proposed business ventures, many of which were very exciting and innovative. When asked to give the reasons why they wanted to start their own business all of them said they wanted to be independent and free to build their own futures.

But when asked about how they viewed profit, they all without exception said that profit was not their primary motivation for starting their businesses. They all agreed that fun and freedom were their chief motivational goals, and most of them said they felt uncomfortable with the idea of profit, seeing it as a sort of first cousin to greed. This is a shame because in a well-run ethical business there is no relationship between profit and greed.

THE GREED MYTH

Unfortunately when you mention the word 'profit' today you risk been labelled as greedy, arrogant, and out-for-yourself.

But the fact is that without profit you can't, and won't, survive. Profit is what secures you and your business's future. Rather than think of it in greedy terms, look at it as if you were putting your hard-earned money into some form of high-earning interest or investment account. You're not just putting your earnings in, you're also putting in your time – lots of it – and you are taking on risk, because every business involves a certain amount of risk.

So your investment comprises:

◆ your money
◆ your time
◆ you taking an amount of risk.

Time
If all you want is a return on your investment of time, then you're probably better off working for an employer because at least your time will be paid for and you won't have the same risks associated with starting and running a business.

Money

This book is about turning your hobby into a profitable business without sinking your life-savings, equity or other funds into it. The aim is to achieve your goals using as little money as possible. However, you will still be investing some money, be it on having a website built, marketing, product development etc.

It's only logical and fair that if you invest money into something you get a return. This return should be greater than if you simply put your money in a savings account, because by investing money in your business you are taking a greater risk than in a savings account.

Risk

By starting your own business you are taking a risk. Hopefully by using the strategies in this book you can minimise your risk but there will always be a danger you won't recoup your initial investment.

So profit is your return for investing *time* and *money* in your business and taking a certain amount of *risk*.

The difference between greed and profit

On the other hand, *greed* comes into the equation when you charge more than you should be charging and somehow have either managed to con people into buying from you or alternatively be in a situation where these people have no choice but to use your products or services.

We all know of businesses who earn what can only be described as obscene profits, but few of these businesses continue to earn these profits for very long, because soon competition enters the market and prices and profits are driven down.

The KTE philosophy isn't about greed. We're not about exploiting or deceiving – we're about running ethical businesses that satisfy needs where our customers are happy they've found our products and services and we have fun providing these and earn profit doing so.

SUMMARY

1. Any hobby has the potential to be turned into a profitable business provided you seek out the real opportunity.

2. Successful Kitchen Table Entrepreneurs are those who are making a living from what they love doing; completely self-reliant and self-motivated; work to written goals; see opportunity in everything and never take rejection personally.

3. The KTE philosophy is all about fun, freedom and profit.

4. There's nothing greedy or distasteful about making profit. Profit is the reward for your investment in terms of time, money and risk.

2

Getting Great Ideas

WHERE TO GET GREAT IDEAS

As I said earlier, it's vital to explore all of the possibilities that your hobby presents. Often the greatest ideas won't be immediately apparent, which is why we need to have some sort of strategy for unlocking them.

By far the most difficult way of coming up with ideas is to sit down with a blank piece of paper and try to think of things.

My favourite methods are:

- ◆ looking for ideas while enjoying my hobby
- ◆ brainstorming
- ◆ readers' letters.

Looking for ideas while enjoying your hobby

By far the easiest, and I believe the most enjoyable way of getting your creative juices flowing is to get out there and throw yourself into your hobby.

But rather than just enjoy yourself I want you to think about what frustrates you most about your hobby. You see, very often the best business opportunities lie in what we don't like about something.

◆ EXPERIENCE ◆

Every dog lover will know how frustrating dog leads have been. In the past, all you could buy were short leads that meant your dog often pulled one way and you the other.

The problem was finally solved when someone came up with the simple idea of the retractable dog lead, which meant that at last you could let your dog walk in the direction they wanted to while still being on their lead. And if you don't want your dog to walk any further you simply apply a brake using your finger. When your dog walks closer to you the lead retracts back into its housing.

But why did it take us so long to get this simple tool?

I'm convinced the reason is that those who manufacture dog leads never actually walked a dog themselves, because the only person who could have come up with such a product is someone who has long suffered the frustrating limitations of the traditional dog lead.

◆ EXPERIENCE ◆

Gardening can be really back-breaking work. A much-needed improvement for gardeners came about when one garden tool manufacturer introduced a new range of gardening tools.

These included such things as spades with extra-long handles, clipping shears with cushions to stop your elbows from getting jarred when you used them, and lightweight seats set at specially low heights to allow you to weed while sitting down.

Again, just like the modified dog lead, the reason these tools became overnight successes was they were designed by people who gardened, who believed their favourite pastime could be made more enjoyable and less painful by adding a few thoughtful modifications to the original products.

So ask yourself:

What's the one thing you find most frustrating about your hobby?

The 'thing' needn't even be connected to your hobby. For example let's say you're a keen walker and you find the maps you're using difficult to store comfortably when you're walking, or hard to keep dry in the rain.

For an entrepreneur this type of problem represents opportunities.

◆ You could design a map that suits the particular needs of your hobby, and either publish your own maps or approach map companies with your ideas on how their product can be improved, and offer your services as a consultant.

◆ You could come up with some sort of carrying case that makes it easier to store maps and read them in the rain.

◆ If one is already available elsewhere in the world you could apply to the manufacturers for a distributor's licence to sell the product here in the UK.

◆ If it's already available in the UK, you could investigate buying the product wholesale and maybe offering it as one item in a mail order business.

Identify the problem and find an easy way of solving it.

Brainstorming

Brainstorming is another way of coming up with fresh and innovative ideas. In its simplest form it involves you sitting down and writing down every idea that comes into your head on a given subject. It doesn't matter what you write down, as the objective of the exercise is to 'storm' the right-hand side of your brain – the creative side – while ignoring any signals from the left-hand side of your brain – the side that deals with logic and order.

Although an extremely effective way of generating ideas, if you're new to this technique it might take you a little time to get used to it. So don't be despondent if it doesn't work for you. Stick with it and I promise it'll pay dividends.

You may find the following 'rules' and techniques helpful, but do whatever you're comfortable with and fairly soon you'll reap the rewards.

'Rules' for brainstorming

1. Do not judge any of your ideas.

2. Write down everything that comes into your head regardless of how silly or irrelevant it may sound.

3. The exercise is all about quantity, and not quality.

4. Work in five-minute bursts, stop, and then do something else for a few minutes before starting again.

5. Don't do it if you're tired or irritable. This technique works better when you're fresh and in a positive frame of mind.

Techniques for brainstorming

1. On a large, blank piece of paper write down a number of key words associated with your hobby. For example if your hobby is fishing you could write down: fishing rod, fish, hook, bait, fishing boat, beach, pier etc.

2. Allow yourself to go wild with your ideas and remember not to judge/ evaluate anything you write down. As soon as you get an idea down on paper move on to the next one.

3. Use pictures to generate ideas. Open any page of your favourite hobby magazine, look at the pictures, and write down whatever comes into your head.

4. Use questions to generate ideas. Six great questions to get going on are: How?, Why?, Where?, When?, Who?, What?.

5. Don't take this too seriously. Try to think of some funny ideas and write them down. For example if you're hobby is water-skiing, imagine the Queen learning to water ski with Prince Phillip being towed behind in a doughnut.

6. Use a stopwatch to time your five-minute session and as soon it ends, STOP.

What can you expect at the end of a session?
Given time to master this technique, you'll find that you start coming up with some exciting potential business ideas. But I stress that just like any other worthwhile technique it takes time and patience before you get the best out of it.

If you find after trying it a number of times that you're still getting nothing – don't despair. Take a break from it and come back to it later when you're fresh and make sure you use all the techniques above. I find pictures a great help. It's amazing what looking at just one picture can do for your imagination.

Readers' letters

The readers' letters section of your hobby magazine and the online forums and message boards for your hobby websites are fantastic places to get new ideas for your business.

Browse through them and you'll start to see common moans, usually directed at manufacturers and suppliers who are perceived as failing to satisfy their customers' needs. It's a great place to find out what others are thinking and what people would really like to buy.

Most large businesses work on economies of scale and will only introduce a product or service if they're sure there'll be a large enough demand to justify full-scale production. Often this reluctance creates an ideal opportunity for a creative entrepreneur to hop in and plug the gap in the market.

In my own gardening business I regularly read online forums and the letters in gardening magazines and have found it to be enormously helpful when planning marketing campaigns and finding out what customers really want.

◆ EXPERIENCE ◆

When I started studying the letters pages of one of the gardening magazines I subscribe to, I began to notice that certain readers' questions kept coming up in the spring, usually from readers who were new to gardening and wanted to know how to plan their first garden. From this information I launched my first gardening course – *How to plan your first garden* which I run in springtime.

◆ TIP ◆

Some hobby magazines also have a readers' tips section, which can be full of useful ideas on creating innovative products.

But beware of sharing your top tips with anyone else. A couple of years ago a reader of a sailing magazine I subscribe to submitted a simple solution for safeguarding an outboard motor against theft. To his surprise, and I believe understandable annoyance, he later saw an exact replica of his device on sale at the Southampton Boat Show. When he enquired further about the origins of the product the salesman told him his company had got the idea for the product from a reader's tip in a sailing magazine.

The company in question is one of the largest in the world and is selling thousands of these gadgets worldwide without paying a penny to the original inventor.

If you are developing a prototype product you should look to have it patented to stop this from happening. To do this you'll need to get specialist advice from a solicitor who deals with this sort of thing.

KEEPING A NOTEBOOK

Ideas are like jokes – you can never remember the good ones. So it's essential to record everything you come up with in a notebook. Personally I prefer to use an A4, hardback, spiral-bound notebook, which I keep safely at home. I use a small pocket-sized notebook when I'm out and later transfer my notes into my master notebook when I get home.

Some tips for keeping a notebook:

- Find a notebook that you're happy with and then as soon as you fill one book buy the same type of notebook so when you come to filing them on a shelf they'll fit together. This way there's less chance of you losing your information.

- Use your notebook to record everything about your intended hobby business.

- Record all your ideas in your notebook, even those you don't like.

- Always be on the lookout for contacts. For example, names and addresses of businesses that make things you might need for your business etc.

- When you come across an interesting magazine or newspaper feature, cut it out and paste it into your notebook.

- Using your PC as a notebook is fine. Just make sure you back it up on either a disk or CD.

EVALUATING YOUR IDEAS

As someone once said, great ideas only work if you do.

While undoubtedly true, this doesn't mean that every idea you come up with, regardless of how you work on it, will bear fruit.

Neither should you get frustrated if some of your ideas seem to be too far-fetched at this stage.

Instead, see your ideas as doorways to your future business. Some you can open today; others may have to wait until you have sufficient resources to put them into action; and a few doors you won't be able to open at all until you do a bit more research.

Regardless of how many potential ideas you come up with for turning your hobby into a business you'll need to have some sort of system for evaluating them.

Generally there are three areas you'll need to consider:

1. your resources
2. your lifestyle
3. feasibility.

YOUR RESOURCES

However brilliant your idea may seem you will only be capable of starting it if you have adequate resources.

Be brutally honest with yourself here. It's no good starting something and then finding that you haven't got what it takes to continue with your venture.

Finance

Unfortunately too many new businesses fail simply because their owners hadn't forecasted how much it was all going to cost to get started and survive the first and often difficult months trading that face every new business.

Skills

Unless you've got enormous financial backing for your venture you're probably going to have to do everything yourself. This means being able to negotiate with suppliers, sell to customers and be shrewd with the books.

There are lots of places to get help from. You can either buy specialist books written entirely on sales, bookkeeping etc, or you can go on courses.

Regardless of your experience you should contact your local Enterprise Centre where you'll find a wide range of courses specifically run for people starting their own businesses with little or no previous experience.

The courses are subsidised by the government so the fees are affordable.

YOUR LIFESTYLE

Ignore this one at your peril! Starting your own business is one of the most exciting things you can do. Get it right and you'll never have to work for anyone again. You'll also enjoy the enormous satisfaction that comes with building and securing your own future.

But, and here's the but!

Starting your own business comes with responsibilities that you might find are incompatible with your lifestyle.

If, like many people, you're the type of person who values your free time and never wants to work weekends, and the business you're planning to start will only work at weekends, then obviously you have a problem. One of the top dream businesses that people imagine themselves working at is running their own seaside guesthouse. Just imagine waking up every morning with a fresh breeze blowing through your chocolate box rose-adorned cottage. While you prepare breakfast your guests wait in patient anticipation complimenting your carefully chosen colour scheme. Unfortunately the reality is something different and there will undoubtedly be occasions where running this type of business means you have little time to enjoy where you're living.

Don't do what most people do and adopt the, 'It'll be ok, I'll be able to hire people to cover weekends,' attitude because this won't work. If your business idea will only work at times when you don't want to work at it then find another opportunity.

To succeed you'll need to be able to devote 100 per cent to your business, at least in the crucial early make or break period.

FEASIBILITY

Before you invest time and money in any business idea you must be sure that what you're proposing is feasible.

Later we'll look at what's involved in working out cash flow and profit and loss forecasts for your business. We'll also look at formulas for calculating how much you need to charge for your products or services. But before you get to this stage get into the habit of looking at your ideas in terms of how feasible they actually are – and don't make the same mistake as my Christmas tree seller.

◆ EXPERIENCE ◆

A guy I know had an idea. He was going to sell Christmas trees from an area in front of his local pub.

The pub, located on a busy road, had a large grassed area which made an ideal sales area for him to set up his seasonal shop. I was intrigued to find out more as his idea seemed to be based on the KTE spirit.

However, when I spoke to him about his business, what became apparent was that he hadn't really given the idea much thought. He told me he was going to run his operation on a Monday to Friday basis as these were the only days the pub would allow him to use their car park. Weekends, he was told, were too busy for them to give up valuable parking space, which in my view meant he'd lost the two best days of the week.

Another problem facing his business was his lack of foresight in relation to costs versus profit.

When I asked him how many trees he was expecting to sell a week, he didn't know. A day? No idea. Over the whole period? Again no idea. All he could tell me was that he had committed himself to buying a minimum of 20 trees a week and he was going to be there for three weeks.

So if he cleared all his stock he would sell a total of 60 trees.

He had two size trees available. Small ones retailed at £7.95 and large ones at £11.95.

Now I don't know how much he paid for them, but even if he got them all free and sold them all – 50% small trees and 50% large trees, his profit and loss would look something like this:

30 trees $\times$ £11.95 = £358.50

30 trees $\times$ £ 7.95 = £238.50

Total sales £597.00

Assuming that his only costs were his time, which is extremely unlikely, his weekly amount would be £199.

He arrived every morning at 9.00am and finished at 5.00pm. So his total hourly rate for the week would be £4.97.

Of course he could have sold much more than his minimum figures and could have earned far more.

However, I believe this would have been difficult as all of his trees dropped their needles. He didn't seem to see this as a problem, but I know having spent a number of Christmas holidays continually hoovering up needles that I would never buy the type of tree that Alan was selling.

I also prefer, as many others do now, to buy the now very popular living tree that can be planted once the holiday is over.

When I raised these points with Alan, he told me I was being too fussy. So I asked him how many trees he'd sold. 'Well none, yet,' he said. 'But it's early days.'

Despite all this Alan was an agreeable, likeable guy whose entrepreneurial spirit was admired. Especially the way he'd stand out on the grassed area for five, long cold days in the run up to Christmas.

So he did manage to sell trees?

How many he sold we'll never know but I think Alan would now agree that his idea would have been far better if he'd subjected it to some sort of feasibility study.

Conducting a simple feasibility study

When you're working through your ideas get into the habit of having a calculator to hand and working out very quick, rounded-off figures, just like I did for Alan's business. Test your idea on a best scenario basis followed by a worse case scenario.

Let's say you're planning to run walking holidays.

So you work out very roughly what you're hoping to charge your customers, taking into account all the costs you're going to incur. Your basic costs should include provisions for:

- marketing
- stationery, brochures etc
- public liability insurance
- salary costs, including a provision for hiring in additional staff if you think you'll need them
- stock if applicable.

I stress you're making rough calculations here. You don't need to work in the cost of every nut and bolt. Just try to be as realistic as you can, being generous with your allowances for expenditure.

◆ TIP ◆

One of the things I've learnt from running my own businesses is that things always seem to cost far more than I initially think they will.

Armed with some rough figures you're ready to work out three useful and very difficult scenarios.

1. Best case scenario.
2. Worst case scenario.
3. Most likely case scenario.

Best case scenario

For your best case scenario work out how many holidays you could actually run, given your resources in terms of time, money etc.

What have you come up with?

For example, if the net amount you're hoping to earn per customer, per holiday, is £80, and given your resources in terms of time available etc, the most holidays you can expect to sell is 100, then that means at the best case you'll earn £8,000.

Are you happy with the amount of the effort you're going to have put in?

If you are, great – obviously you've got an idea worth continuing with. However if your figures are disappointing it doesn't necessarily mean that your idea is unworkable. At this stage all you've worked out is that in its present form it's not going to be sufficient to make a profitable business.

Had Alan undertaken some sort of feasibility study with his Christmas tree shop he would have discovered that he needed to sell additional product lines to succeed. There are all sorts of things he could have sold with his trees: decorations, stands, holly wreaths, flower arrangements etc.

He could also have boosted his sales by offering his customers a service where he would collect and dispose of their trees after the Christmas holidays.

As Christmas trees are what is classified as 'green recyclable' waste, he wouldn't even need to apply for a waste carrier's licence from the Environment Agency. All he'd need is to find a trade waste recycling centre and set aside a couple of days to collect and dispose of his trees.

Worst case scenario

Don't forget to calculate a worst case scenario. My favourite way of doing this is to imagine I'll sell nothing.

Obviously this is the sort of scenario we all hope will never happen and provided you undertake sufficient market research before you invest any of your money, it should never arise.

However there will always be factors outside of your control which could destroy even the most carefully-laid business plans. For example, who could have foreseen the impact that the foot and mouth crisis would have had on local tourist business? Many of the walking holiday companies went out of business because most of the countryside in their areas was closed to the public.

Despite investing in advertising and successfully filling their holiday bookings they ended up with no customers and therefore no revenue.

Thankfully this sort of scenario is rare, but it's worth taking a bit of time to ask yourself what would happen if the business you're planning to start had no customers.

How would you survive?

Is the potential financial loss that you would suffer something that you can bear, or would you end up losing everything?

If it's the case that you would end up losing you might like to revise your plans so as to reduce your risk.

Most likely scenario
All being well this is the scenario you most likely expect to achieve. although it's impossible to predict exact expenditure and sales figures, you should be able to work out what you think is possible.

Again if the figures you come up with during this scenario fall below what's needed to make your idea worthwhile then either re-work your idea or start afresh.

> Get into the habit of working out feasibilities for everything you come up with. Not only is it a brilliant way of coming up with new ideas, but you're also starting to think like an entrepreneur.

Don't limit your feasibility studies to your own business ideas. It's always interesting to look at what other entrepreneurs are doing. You'll soon start to see businesses that are doomed from the start, and hopefully learn from others' successful business ideas.

Your findings

Regardless of how brilliant, innovative or otherwise your idea might seem to be, it must be:

◆ capable of making enough money to make it a worthwhile investment in terms of your time and money. This needn't be immediate, provided there is some identifiable period in the future when your idea will come into fruition

◆ capable of being started within your current resources in terms of finance, skills and knowledge.

The time spent working out some rough figures and projections at this early stage is time well spent and will highlight the strengths and weaknesses of your idea.

Don't be despondent if your initial ideas don't come up to your expectations. Now is the time to find that out. Better to suffer the disappointment now and get on with building new ideas than end up at some time in the future with a hopelessly loss-making venture.

HOBBY BUSINESS IDEAS

Most hobbies can find an opportunity somewhere in the following ten business models.

My advice is that you read through the following list with an open mind. Don't dismiss anything immediately. Simply read through them all a number of times and then write them down on a piece of card or in your notebook. Then in the next few days, whenever you get a moment, start working through this list and seeing how many businesses you could start from your hobby.

Remember that most successful KTEs have more than one business. They don't risk their futures on one venture, but rather have a number of smaller independent businesses on the go at any one time. So even if you have already decided on the structure of your proposed business, don't be afraid to let your imagination run riot and see what else you can achieve.

Sales business

Probably the most common of all business models – this is where you either buy in a product wholesale or make your own product and then retail it.

Examples of this type of business are antiquarian book dealers, craft shops, art dealers, antique dealers etc.

Service business

A service business is one where you either sell your own skills, for example a gardener offering a gardening service, or you offer a business where you employ others and market their skills.

Examples of service businesses are: gardening services, dog walking services, interior design services, garden design service.

You could also consider employing others.

Another way is to employ others, and then 'rent out' their skills and experience. For example in our gardening business we employ people to a do a range of things including gardening, teaching and designing. Essentially we 'rent' their skills and sell them to our clients earning a profit on what we pay them and what we charge our clients.

Tuition business

Regardless of what hobby you're interested in, there will always be new enthusiasts joining who will want to find out as much as they can about their new hobby.

The business opportunity here is to organise classes and courses so that both newcomers and those with some experience can learn the ropes.

Examples of tuition businesses include organising and running creative writing courses, fishing courses, cookery courses, flower arranging and craft making courses, candle making courses.

You don't have to be an expert yourself to start and run this type of business. Provided you are a skilled organiser and capable of advertising and marketing your courses you can employ teachers or those with specialist knowledge to give your courses.

For example, I run gardening courses and never have any difficulty finding suitably qualified teachers for my classes.

Activity business

Hobbies offer unlimited business opportunities for anyone with organisational skills.

The sort of businesses we're looking at here are organising painting holidays, creative writing holidays, walking holidays, sailing holidays, tours to public gardens, and/or places of interest, deep sea angling trips.

The possibilities are endless here and the great thing about this type of business is that all you really need to get started is your kitchen table. For example, if you're planning to run creative writing holidays you don't need to have your own B&B, hotel or venue to run them from. All you need is to find suitable hotels or venues to run your courses from, negotiate the best deal you can with the proprietors, and organise your holidays.

Exhibition business

This is a business where you arrange local, national and/or online exhibitions of work.

It is particularly suitable if your hobby involves photography, painting, flower arranging, crafts, candle making etc.

Your revenue comes from charging your exhibitors fees to exhibit at your shows, and/or commission on what they sell.

Wholesaling

Rather than simply retail products, you could also become a wholesaler. It's worth investigating to see what products you could import and then sell to the UK market.

There are a number of international trade fairs held annually where you can meet and find businesses looking for agents for their products.

The secret with this type of business is to steer away from the main products of your hobby and look for those things that people have difficulty finding. Products that the larger businesses will ignore as they don't believe they can sell them in large enough quantities to justify their expenditure.

Competitions

You can run all sorts of hobby-based competitions, for example painting competitions, creative writing competitions, poetry competitions, photography competitions.

Revenue comes from charging entrance fees, a portion of which then goes as prize money.

Whilst not a huge business on its own, running competitions can be an excellent way of generating publicity for your business while earning a modest income.

Information sharing

Information sharing business is where you sell information regarding your particularly hobby or interest.

Examples of this type of business:

- Setting up a website where you list all the events that would be of interest to those participating in your hobby and charging a membership or subscription fee.

- Publishing your own guide books or annual directories listing all the information about your particular hobby.

- Publishing your own regular magazine or newsletter.

Hire business

Whatever your hobby, the chances are there will be something you can rent out to other hobby enthusiasts.

Examples of this type of business include cycle hire business, fishing rod hire, boat hire, photography equipment hire, holiday home hire, tents and camping equipment hire, garden furniture hire, pot plant hire for offices, hotels, residential homes, stage and movie props.

A hire service can be an excellent way of generating additional revenue for a traditional sales business. Let's say you've opened a cycle shop – why not offer cycle hire as well?

Whatever you're planning to sell – what can you hire to boost your sales?

If you're a classic car collector, could you hire your vehicles out to film companies?

Or if you're an outdoor caterer could you also include a glass hire service in your business?

THE BEST PLACE TO START FROM

As I said earlier, the best place to start your business is from where you're standing at the moment.

Kitchen Table Entrepreneurship is all about travelling light and not committing to expensive leases, garage loads of expensive stock, costly franchise agreements and the like.

Every successful entrepreneur has started from where you're standing now. In all probability many haven't even had as much as you do – so don't think because you think you have nothing at the moment you can't start a successful business. You can. All you need to do is start working with what you have from wherever you are right now.

◆ TIP ◆

Capitalise on your strengths and manage your weaknesses.

INTRODUCING YOU TO YOUR MOST IMPORTANT CLIENT

Before we finish this chapter I want to introduce you to your most important client – YOU.

You are your business's most important client, something often overlooked and even frowned at by many small business owners.

Rather than satisfy their own needs they crucify themselves trying to satisfy the needs of others. When eventually it all gets too much for them they close their door, bitter and defeated by the whole experience.

I don't believe this should be the case and before you go any further with your business ideas I want you to sign a pact. I want you to promise yourself that the real reason you are starting your own business is to satisfy your needs first. Of course your needs also includes those closest to you: husband, wife, partner and children.

What's important is you accept now that unless you satisfy your own needs, you cannot begin to satisfy your potential customers.

You can vary the following pact to suit your own personal circumstances.

I am my business's most important customer.

Because I am my business's most important customer, I will look after myself. I will treat myself with respect. I will listen to my inner needs and not run myself down so much as I'm too tired to work effectively.

Neither will I let my new business take over my life to such an extent that I am no longer free to enjoy myself or spend time with those that mean the most to me.

Signed _____ Dated _____

From now on promise to look after yourself; to hold yourself in the same esteem you would someone you consider to be your business's best customer.

Of course this doesn't mean opting out of the hard work that lies ahead. Or taking as much time off as you want or spending money you don't have. But it does mean looking after yourself and making sure that the business you're planning to start satisfies your needs, which means:

- if you don't like working weekends, then don't start a business that involves working weekends

- if you really don't like people, don't start a business which revolves around other people. Start a mail order business instead when ordering is done online and most of the time your business runs without you ever really having direct customer contact except for written correspondence.

Now is the time to identify your needs. Not a few months from now when you've invested your money, opened your business and discovered that it's actually not for you at all.

The Kitchen Table Entrepreneur philosophy is all about fun, freedom and profit, realising your dreams and achieving your goals. This can only be achieved by recognising that you are in fact your business's most important customer. You are also your business's greatest asset.

SUMMARY

1. Getting ideas is simply a process of looking at things differently and working through lots of different ideas until you find the gems hidden in the sand.

2. Try to see if your idea fits into the hobby business ideas as these business models represent enormous potential.

3. Be prepared to start from where you are right now. If your dream is to run a florists' shop, but you can't afford to buy one or take on a shop lease, then be prepared to start with a bucket, selling door-to-door.

3

What's Involved in
Starting Your Business

As soon as you've got your ideas together you will need to get a framework from which to start your business.

These are the main areas that you need to consider when starting your business:

- Naming your business.
- Deciding where to base your business.
- Complying with the law.
- Deciding on a trading identity for your business.
- Deciding whether or not to register for VAT.

In Chapter 9, we look at what's involved in deciding which trading identity would be suitable for your business and also look at what's involved in VAT. My advice is for you to read Chapter 9 when you feel ready for it. For now though, let's look at some things you'll need to consider when christening your new business and where your new venture is going to live.

DECIDING ON A NAME FOR YOUR BUSINESS

Choosing the right name for your business is important and is something you need to really think about because whatever name you give to your business will need to create the right image for potential customers.

Let's say you're planning to organise painting holidays in Cornwall. You could call your business simply 'Painting Holidays in Cornwall', but the obvious problem here is that it doesn't give any more information than the obvious.

Before you go any further you need to ask yourself more questions about your proposed business:

- Are your holidays aimed at the budget-conscious artist looking for cheap hostel-type accommodation with arranged visits to local beauty sites. Or at would-be artists looking for a luxury break, which includes painting tuition and pampering?

- Where in Cornwall are your holidays based?

- What's your own painting expertise?

- Are painting holidays the only holidays you're intending to run or will you include other holidays at some future date, such as creative writing courses?

Obviously you are never going to be able to answer all of these questions with the name of your business, but you can improve on the initial name by making it less restrictive and more imaginative.

One of the problems with the original name is that it concentrates on two words – 'painting' and 'holiday'.

The difficulty here is that anyone interested in learning how to paint might get the impression that this business runs holidays for seasoned painters and not beginners, while experienced painters might find the word 'holiday' a turn off.

But by far the greatest difficulty is that it limits your business from offering anything other than painting holidays.

So what's the alternative? You could go for something like 'Creative Breaks Cornwall'.

The advantage with this name is that it conjures up a number of intriguing possibilities without taking away from the core business – painting holidays.

You could also include a strap line on your business advertisements, websites etc:

Creative Breaks Cornwall
Discovering the artist within

If and when you decide to offer other types of holidays your business name is not going to hold you back.

Your business name doesn't have to describe your business

Your business name doesn't have to describe or even suggest what your business offers.

Take Amazon as an example. Here we have the world's largest retailer of books with no mention of books anywhere in the company name. Yet everyone knows they retail books. Although originally marketed as an online book retailer, Amazon now sells a whole range of non-book products including software and games.

The advantage of choosing a name like Amazon is that not only is it easy to remember and intriguing, but the name doesn't restrict the future growth or diversity of the business. Richard Branson's Virgin Group is similar.

 ◆ TIP ◆

Be imaginative and make sure whatever name you choose doesn't restrict your future business by pigeon-holing you into something that's too narrow.

Beware of choosing cliché names

It's also a good idea to avoid choosing a cliché business name. By this I mean something like Green Fingers Gardening Company or Joe's Bloomers, or Harriet's Heavenly Pastries etc.

While names like these might seem like a good idea at the time just wait until you discover there's already more than one of them in the country and suddenly your business isn't unique after all.

Bargain hunting

The exception to the rule is when you're absolutely certain that what you're offering is going to be cheaper than offered by most other retailers, you should include this information somewhere in your title.

Let's say you're planning to open an online fishing tackle shop where offering rock bottom prices is the basis of your marketing strategy.

The Fisherman's Warehouse
Cheapest tackle online

Choosing to use a word like 'warehouse' as opposed to 'shop' suggests large quantities at low prices.

Personalising the name

You could also personalise your business name and call it something like Joe's Fisherman's Warehouse.

Some businesses are ideal for this sort of personalisation, particularly if they involve looking after something that your customer treasures, like children, pets, gardens etc.

While John Browne's Dog Walking Service might seem boring and unimaginative, it does suggest to potential customers that John Browne and not someone unknown to them will be looking after their dog. Including your own name in your business name can under the right circumstances create a feeling of trust, which brings credibility. So don't be afraid to include your own name particularly if the business you're planning to run involves looking after other people's treasures.

Other factors

Is the business name you want actually available?
There is no absolute right to a business name unless of course that name is the name of a company or another business trading in the same area as you're intending to.

So if there's already a Flo's Dog Walking Service or Martin's Organic Vegetables in your area then obviously were you to start up a similar business using the same name they would have a legal argument to say that you are trading using their name.

Of course it would also be silly to knowingly use another business name as not only are you bound for legal conflict, you are also denying your business any opportunity of being unique.

 TIP ◆

One of the easiest ways to check whether anyone is already using your name is to surf the Internet, which is a good idea anyway because when it comes to creating a website for your business you want to be sure that the domain name you want is available.

Search through as many search engines as you can, including, Yahoo!, Google, Ask Jeeves and any web directories relating to your chosen field.

Don't get too despondent if you find your name is already being used by another business. Better to find this out now than when you've ordered all your stationery, brochures and the like.

When you've decided on your name, ask yourself:

- Will it fit comfortably on your stationery. For example if you're planning to have labels printed for your products, will the name fit on a small label?

- Will it create the right image for your business?

- Will it build trust and credibility?

- Can you get a website domain name to fit in with your business name?

- If your business expands, diversifies or changes completely, can you keep this name or will another be needed?

- If you abbreviate your name, what do you get. For example, my gardening business is called Paul Power Landscapes, which abbreviates to PPL. Can your name be abbreviated, and if so are you comfortable with the abbreviation?

OPENING A BUSINESS BANK ACCOUNT

There is no legal requirement that I am aware of that says you must have a business bank account. However, there are banking terms and conditions, which if you ever have the time and patience to read will tell you that you cannot use your personal account for business banking.

Operating without a business bank account – cash only

If you're planning to run a small hobby business where all of your customers can pay you in cash then you don't necessarily have to open a bank account.

You could manage your money by simply paying it into a cash till, which you then record as business income. You keep a float in your till to pay your business bills etc, and then finally you pay yourself using cash.

Because this money has now effectively gone from being business cash to personal drawings, I can't see why any bank can object when you lodge this money as it is after all your wages. Not business income!

Obviously there'll only be a limited amount of businesses that will want to operate on this sort of basis and with credit card usage becoming more and more popular it looks like cash will become a thing of the past.

What to look for in a business bank

At the time of writing there are four main high street banks and I believe all of them offer more or less the same thing. Certainly their charges are similar and once you get past any initial period of free banking, there's not much difference.

◆ **EXPERIENCE** ◆

The bank our businesses are with gives us free banking provided we operate our account within certain restrictions, which include a limit to how many lodgements we can make.

I've found the 'limits' to be more than generous and if you do exceed your limit you then only pay to lodge those items over the pre-agreed quota.

But there's a drawback: cash. Our free banking account is basically a postal bank where the only way to lodge monies is either via the post using their prepaid envelopes or in an envelope using one of their branch's cash dispensers, which means lodging cash is pretty impossible.

However this suits our business as most of our payments are either made by cheque or credit card and the small amount of cash we do get we can use as petty cash.

These arrangements suit us but might not suit your business. Shop around and get the best package for your business.

Ask yourself:

1. Are you looking for a bank account to simply lodge and withdraw money, or are you looking for a bank where you will need to apply for overdrafts, loans etc?

2. Are you planning to take credit cards?

3. Will you be taking large amounts of cash?

4. Will you buying your products from abroad?

5. Will you be hiring staff?

If you answer yes to most or all of the above questions then you're going to need a business bank as opposed to simply a business bank account.

Anyone who is considering future borrowings for their business, employing staff and taking large amounts of cash will need a bank where they can actually speak to a business bank advisor who will be sympathetic to the sort of problems you face.

◆ **EXPERIENCE** ◆

The owner of a small cleaning business lodged a number of cheques into her business bank account. Unfortunately she failed to make sure the cheques had actually cleared before writing cheques for her employees' wages. She believed she'd left plenty time before writing her salary cheques.

The results were disastrous. The cheques bounced, which meant her employees hadn't been paid. This started a panic with staff telling her customers that they thought her business had gone bankrupt. It might as well have done because staff were now unwilling to work and customers' offices not cleaned.

It was difficult for her to rebuild her business but she did. The bank, as you would expect, dismissed her complaint telling her that it was her responsibility to ensure she had sufficient funds in her account prior to writing her cheques. Her argument was that her cheques had taken an extraordinarily long time to clear.

Situations like this can arise when you run your own business so it's important that you choose a bank that you are comfortable with, and most importantly that you have a named contact in that bank who you can speak to and is familiar with your business.

Ask your bank manager some questions

Someone once described a bank manager as being: 'someone who loans you an umbrella when it's sunny, then asks for it back when it rains.' This bears out my own personal experiences!

Before committing yourself to opening your business account you should ask prospective banks as many questions as you can. The list below is by no means exhaustive:

1. Will you have your own personal contact within their bank who you can call on for help and advice?

2. What is their criteria for granting business overdrafts? Some banks will insist you have an established track record with them for a period before they will consider your application.

3. Ask them to explain their bank charges, particularly in relation to free banking offers. Most banks only offer free banking on the basis that you manage your account within certain parameters. If you exceed those limits will you have to pay charges on all your transactions or just those that exceed their limits?

4. Ask them how they can help your business. This is where you'll find out if you're talking to a member of staff in a call centre reading from a crib sheet or someone who is actually interested in working with your business.

Finally, remember that banks exist to make profit for their shareholders.

 ◆ TIP ◆

When it comes to bank accounts – keep your personal and business accounts at separate banks.

While it might seem like a good idea to keep your personal bank account and business bank account with the same bank, I'd advise against it.

The reason I recommend you keep your accounts at separate banks or building societies is that in the event that you have a problem with one account, the bank may, at its discretion, enforce its power and put a freeze on your other accounts thus rendering you completely impotent.

Let's say, for example, that you find yourself in the same situation as the proprietor of the cleaning company I told you about earlier. Were you to find yourself in this unfortunate situation it's quite probable that the bank would freeze your personal account as well as your business bank account, which as you can imagine would even be more disastrous.

Believe me, in business things can always get worse!

Despite your best efforts there may be times when either your customers let you down or an unforeseen bill presents itself and suddenly you find yourself overdrawn beyond your limits. Before you know it everything is frozen.

Contingency plan your banking by having a number of bank accounts with different banks or building societies.

CREATING A BUSINESS IDENTITY

Telephone lines

Do you need another line? Yes, I believe you do. Nothing will put potential customers off more than a badly answered telephone. In the past I've phoned businesses where children have answered the phone and I've given up trying to get them to put mum or dad on so I can order something. Instead I've done what most people would do – moved on.

A separate business line will not only give your business credibility, but also make life easier for you. When the phone rings you know it's business.

The disadvantage to having a separate business line is, of course, cost. Telephone providers charge more for a business line than they do a domestic, but I believe that this cost is a relatively small price to pay to give your business an enhanced professional image. By using a domestic line as opposed to a business line you miss out on free listings in the business section of the phone book and of course when anyone searches directory enquiries you will only be listed if you have a business line. Also, were your line to go down for any reason repairs to business lines get priority over domestic ones.

Freephone numbers

When deciding on a business number you could also consider introducing a freephone number or a number where your customers only pay the cost of local call to contact you. Incentives like these can be useful if you're operating in a competitive environment where potential customers are faced with lots of different companies to choose from.

The fact that your number will cost either nothing to call or the cost of a local call will give them an added incentive to call your business first.

Stationery

Now that you have decided on your trading identity and chosen a suitable name you are ready to create your business identity, which will include things like deciding on a logo for your business and ordering company stationery.

When it comes to publishing stationery you have a number of choices:

♦ Put together your own simple letterhead without a logo and print your own stationery using your PC.

♦ Design your own logos and letterheads either freehand or using a software programme then either print your own stationery or give it to a printer.

♦ Employ a graphic designer to create your logos and letterhead and then either print it yourself or have a printer do it for you.

Your choice of methods will obviously depend on how much money you have available to spend on this. By far the simplest and cheapest way is to do everything yourself. Not every business will need a logo or fancy letterhead and many hobby businesses can get by having their business name, address and telephone number printed somewhere on the page as the example below.

Creative Holidays Cornwall

Primrose Cottage

Seafront

Cornwall

Tel: 12345678

www.chhcs.co.uk

email: info@chhcs.co.uk

Dear Mr Visitor

We have pleasure in enclosing our latest brochure on our painting holidays for this season.

Should you have any questions, or to book your holiday, please call us on the above number or book online using our website.

Thank you for your interest in Creative Holidays Cornwall and we look forward to welcoming you in the not too distant future.

Kind regards

Bill Holiday

Proprietor

Nothing fancy is needed

The important thing when deciding on how to approach your stationery is to remember that nothing fancy is needed. A clean, crisp letterhead is far easier to read than a multi-coloured splurge of print complete with clip art.

Clip art is the image/cartoon graphics you receive free with most software publishing programmes. It should be avoided. If you use it when creating your identity, the chances are that other similar businesses will too.

If you really believe that artwork is crucial to your business success then commission a graphic designer to come up with something brilliant and unique. While clip art is fine for party invitations and birthday announcements, the image of your business will undoubtedly suffer if you use it.

Brochures

For many businesses, brochures are an important marketing tool. Although it's relatively expensive to employ a specialist company to design your brochure, letterhead and so on, it can pay enormous dividends especially if what you're going to be selling is high value and the buyer needs to be assured of your credability.

When a professional designs your brochure you are benefiting not only from their design, but also from their marketing experience.

Before employing a designer to work on your behalf make sure you:

- **See examples of their work.** Not just online; ask them to send you samples so you can determine the quality of the print, paper and get an overall impression of what they're offering.

- **Ask for a written quotation.** Designer's bills are a bit like solicitor's – if left unchecked they can run wildly over your initial budget. Before you enter into any commitment make sure you know exactly what you are getting for your money.

- **Insist on copy-ready proofs.** Hopefully this won't be necessary as professional design companies will always send what is known as 'copy-ready proofs' to you for approval. A CRP is basically a mock-up of how your finished brochure, letterhead or compliment slip will look. It's vital you check these thoroughly for mistakes as once you have given your approval the proofs will be printed and you will have to pay for any amendments or alterations.

◆ **Ask for a credit account.** Some businesses will insist you pay upfront. I don't agree with this as I like to be sure that I'm getting what I pay for. In the event that you're not happy with the quality or you don't get what was originally agreed you will have far more influence if you haven't already settled the bill. The problem you might find is that if you are a new business, designers may be reluctant to undertake the work unless they are convinced they stand a good chance of getting paid for it. If this is the case, offer to pay a deposit on order with the balance falling due when you collect your work. It's also worth asking for an account facility, particularly if you intend using the company for all your future printing requirements.

Before printing anything make sure you check the proofs for errors and omissions. Pay particular attention to things like telephone and fax numbers, website addresses, postcodes and email addresses.

Remember, if you are operating as a sole trader and trading under a different name then by law you must include something like 'Paul Power trading as Walking Holidays Cornwall' on your letterhead. You can do this discreetly by adding it somewhere in the lower header in small print. (See Chapter 9 for more information.)

Small business start-up kits

Many printers now offer an all-in stationery package for new businesses, which usually includes: 250 letterheads, envelopes, business cards and compliments slips.

Provided the quality of print and paper is of an acceptable standard these packages can offer great value for money and in my experience printers are generally happy to include some free artwork and layout.

Prior to confirming your order make sure you ask your printer to show you samples of the type of paper you will be getting and samples of the printing.

Envelopes

When it comes to posting out your letters, brochures, direct sales materials etc, you're going to need to think about envelopes. My advice is that you go with window envelopes. These are the ones where all you have to do is fold your letter in the correct place and the address is automatically displayed through the window. They are particularly useful when you're sending out a mail-shot etc.

◆ TIP ◆

Ask your printer to give you a quote to have your business name printed on your envelopes. Your customers will be more likely to open your letter as they'll recognise your name on the envelope. Otherwise it might get mistaken for junk mail and binned without being opened.

You could also consider hand-writing your envelopes, although depending on your handwriting this can give an amateurish back-bedroom sort of feel to it.

Whatever you decide on make sure everything is consistent.

Which means that you should make sure that:

◆ the colour of the paper matches the colour of the envelope;

◆ the quality of the paper matches the quality of the envelope;

◆ the colour scheme and logos are similar throughout your business – letterheads, website, company vehicles, staff uniforms, business cards etc.

If you're unsure don't commit yourself.

Getting it wrong can be expensive. I've known of small businesses who've rushed their stationery order through only to find something as simple as the telephone number was incorrect. Remember that once you approve the proofs and give your go ahead you have no recourse. The fact that you haven't checked your telephone number, business name or postcode is not the fault of the printers and therefore not only will you end up with the most expensive scrap paper money can buy, but also have to have everything redone.

Always work to a budget.

Starting a business is a bit like organising a wedding. It's so easy for costs to spiral out of control. An extra colour here and little embellishment there, and let's just go for that satin finished paper and suddenly your costs have quadrupled.

The best way to prevent costs getting out of hand is to work out a budget and stick to it.

During your first meeting with your printer let him know what your budget is and make it clear that you will not be spending more than this figure. Provided you've picked a professional printer this won't be a problem. Our printer has been extremely helpful in coming up with novel ways of getting the printing we want done to our budget.

Choosing a printer

It's important to choose a printer that you are comfortable with and someone that you can build up a relationship with. Because I run a number of small businesses, my natural instinct is to choose a similar business to mine to undertake our printing requirements. Once I went to one of those high street printing franchises, and I knew as soon as I walked in the door that the young, disinterested shop assistant who couldn't understand that my surname was Power and not Powers was not going to work out.

Personally I prefer the smaller independent who understands and appreciate the problems that come with running a small business.

YOUR INSURANCE COMPANY

The fact that most Kitchen Table Entrepreneurs will at sometime work from home will have an impact on their home insurance policies. It's important therefore to check with your insurance company that you are covered in the event that someone burgles your home office and steals your computer, printer etc that your cover includes you running your business from home.

Obviously if you're going to be holding stock at home you will also need to ensure that your stock is covered in the event of theft, fire or damage.

Unfortunately the relatively high cost of insurance cover means it's usually one of those things to ignore when starting your own business from home, but you do need to ensure that by running your business from home you don't invalidate your ordinary home contents and buildings insurances.

LOCAL AUTHORITY

Planning regulations generally do not allow private residences to be used for business. So if you're planning to turn your garage into a workshop, you should check with your local planning office to see whether or not you will need planning permission.

However if running your business from home involves little more than working from your kitchen table or spare room then the chances are that nobody will object. But be aware that if you are running a limited company from home the law requires you to display somewhere outside your office the name of your business. You doing this may bring you into conflict with neighbours who may then complain to the local planning officer.

WHERE TO BASE YOUR BUSINESS

It may seem odd that a book promoting the Kitchen Table Entrepreneur advises you to consider working from somewhere other than your home, but there will be times when this will make sense.

Take for example our businesses, which include a general gardening business and cycle hire business.

Our gardening business includes trailers, machinery, vans and all that goes with that. I don't believe that it would be fair on our neighbours to base this sort of thing either outside our home or in our garden. The other problem we'd face is that there is now so much of it we wouldn't be able to fit it all in.

Similarly our cycle business includes bikes and accessories with a need for a small workshop area from where we can service and maintain the bikes. Although our cycle hire business runs from a seafront premises we still need additional storage and workspace.

The solution we found was to rent a unit from where everything is based. The cost of running this unit can be shared proportionately between the business.

But our office is still home based.

The reason for this is that I prefer working from home, and the additional cost of hiring an office on top of workshop/storage space was astronomical. In addition to the costs of hiring office space you also have to pay for water rates, lighting, heating, building insurance, contents insurance, burglar alarms, business rates – which in my mind makes it more sense to be home based.

Of course this arrangement may not suit every business, particularly those employing office-based staff.

If you are planning to rent office space, make sure that you shop around for the best deal and avoid if you can having to agree to a lengthy lease period. Although you may find you get a better rent figure if you agree to a longer let, you might find that after a year the property is no longer suitable for your business and the costs terminating the lease may be so great as to make it impossible.

 TIP ◆

Consider having a home office and a workshop/storage unit elsewhere.

Just like I've done with my businesses you may find that you're better off sourcing some form of cheap storage/workshop area where you can keep stock, machinery etc, and then base your office at home.

Again make sure you work to a budget. Estate agents are paid commission on rent and in my experience will always be pushing towards that 'ideal property', which costs just little bit more than the one you're looking at. Before you know it you've taken on a monthly rent commitment the size of the national debt.

Sharing a unit

It's also worth considering sharing a unit with another business. Obviously you've got be careful who you decide to share with and make sure they're able, and willing, to pay their share of the rent, but doing this can substantially reduce the costs of renting premises.

If you are going to do this make sure you:

◆ get the permission of your landlord. Do this before you agree to rent the property as it's unlikely they'll agree to your sub-letting it once you've moved in;

◆ draw up an agreement detailing who is responsible for what and what happens if one you wants to terminate the agreement;

◆ set up separate standing orders to pay your rent (if your landlord agrees) so that in the event your sharer doesn't pay, your landlord will pursue him and not you.

Although useful for reducing the costs of renting somewhere, you really do need to be sure about whoever you share with.

Small storage units

Gone are the days when renting a storage unit meant you had to take on something the size of a small house. There are now companies who specialise in renting a variety of sizes and who offer easy in-and-out terms, which usually mean that you can rent these units on a weekly or monthly basis. Useful when you're starting out and not sure about how much space you actually need.

The golden rule when it comes to renting anything is not to be tempted to rush into it.

Even if it seems the most idyllic property for your business you should always:

◆ stop and think about it before rushing in and signing on the dotted line;

◆ ask for a copy of the lease agreement, which you then take away with you and read thoroughly before committing. The best place to read lease agreements is away from wherever it is you're planning to rent;

◆ get a solicitor to read the lease for you if the property is anything other than a self-storage type unit.

COMPLYING WITH THE LAW

Unfortunately, small businesses are facing an ever-increasing barrage of legislation and it would be impossible within the scope of this book to cover all possible legalities that you will need to consider. Not every business will be subject to the same laws. For example a business involving food will be subject to different legislation than a business organising water sports.

It's up to you to check what legislation your business will have to adhere to. Ignorance of the law is no defence.

Important legislation you should be aware of if you're planning to open business involving food:

◆ The Food Safety Act 1990
◆ Food Safety (General Food Hygiene) Regulations 1995
◆ Food Safety (Temperature Control) Regulations 1995

You can find full details of the requirements of these acts at The Foods Standards Agency Website: http://cleanup.food.gov.uk.

You should also be aware of the legislation covering the following areas:

◆ employing staff
◆ health and safety legislation
◆ Data Protection Act.

Employing staff

The most important thing to know is that all your employees are entitled by law to be given a **Written Statement of Employment** setting out the main particulars of their employment.

You are also required to undertake a number of checks on anyone you intend employing. These will include things such as:

◆ **The prospective employee's age.** Their age will affect the types of work they are allowed to do; the hours they are allowed to work; rates you must pay them.

◆ **Whether or not they are allowed to work in the UK.** You must be sure that their status in the UK allows them to work. If you employ someone who is not allowed to work in UK, you commit an offence and risk being penalised.

◆ **Their skills and aptitude for the job.** You will have to take up references, background checks etc.

Visit the government's Business Link website http://www.businesslink. gov.uk.

You can use their free software tool to create a Written Statement of Employment for all your employees and use their interactive tool to check your legal responsibilities when taking on staff. There is a whole wealth of information on this site concerning all aspects of employment legislation.

HEALTH AND SAFETY

As a business owner you have a legal responsibility for the health and safety of your employees and anyone that may be affected by your business and its activities. You also have a legal responsibility for the impact your business has on the environment.

It's essential you have in place a properly written health and safety policy for your business.

You can get all the answers to your questions by phoning the Health and Safety Information Line on 0870 1545 500, or visiting the website http://www.hse.gov.uk.

DATA PROTECTION ACT

The provisions of the Data Protection Act 1988 will affect most business owners. It works in two ways:

1. By governing the way personal information is used and stored. Personal information would include your customer's addresses, dates of births, telephone numbers etc.

   The Act requires you to follows the eight data protection principles, which state that all data must be:
   – fairly and lawfully processed
   – processed for limited purposes
   – adequate, relevant and not excessive
   – accurate
   – not kept for longer than is necessary
   – processed in line with the data subject's rights
   – secure
   – not transferred to countries outside the EU without adequate protection.

2. By giving all individuals certain rights.
   These rights, which are known as 'right of subject access', give everyone the right to see the information that is being held about them on a computer, and some paper records. This means that if in

the course of your business you record details about your customers, they can request that you provide them with all the information you hold about them.

Make sure that, whatever it is you're recording about your customers, you'd be happy for them to see it.

The information must also be accurate and up to date. For example if you run a walking holidays business where you regularly send information to customers on your mailing list, periodically you would have to make sure that the details you have are correct and up to date. So it's good practice to include a slip with your mailings asking customers to tell you whether or not they still want to receive your information and inform you of any change in their details.

(There are some exceptions to this, for example when the information stored is being used in the detection and prevention of crime.)

Notification

The commissioner maintains a public register of data controllers. Notification is the way in which a data controller's processing details are added to this register.

The data controller could be you, as business owner, or an employee of your business.

Unless you are exempt from Notification, you must notify the commissioner and pay a fee, currently £35, to be added to the register. This is an annual fee. Failure to notify when you are not exempt is a criminal offence.

To find out whether your business will have to Notify telephone the DPR on 01625 545740 or visit their website at http://www.dpr.gov.uk.

The rights of subject access

Because individuals have a right to see the information that is being held about them – the right of subject access – you need to know what to do if an individual makes a request to your business.

If you receive a request you must:

◆ send them the information you hold on them;
◆ tell them why this information is processed and anyone it may be passed to or seen by;
◆ explain the logic in any automated decisions;
◆ deal with their request within 40 days from the date you receive it;

You may charge an administration fee of no more than £10.

Compensation

Be aware that individuals may seek compensation through the courts if they have suffered damage, or damage and distress, because of any contravention of the Act.

As I said earlier, there is a whole raft of legislation that can affect your business and you must be familiar with it all. I really recommend a visit to the Business Link site, which is an invaluable tool for small business owners and entrepreneurs.

SUMMARY

1. Give plenty of thought to the name you're going to give your business. Your business name creates the first impression of your business, therefore it's important to get it right.

2. Choose a base for your business that suits you in terms of affordability and adaptability. There's nothing wrong with the kitchen table.

3. A successful business is impossible without creating credibility. Therefore it's important that you get it right from day one.

4. Get a dedicated business line for your business and make sure it's answered in a business-like way.

5. Research all legislation that might affect your business and be sure to register where appropriate.

4

Research: The Doorway to Success

The two huge mistakes you can make when starting your business are to:

1. First decide on a product or service to sell and then go out and try to find customers to buy what you're offering.

2. Start without a fully-researched business plan.

Deciding on a product first and then looking for customers to buy your goods is a common problem, and the reason many businesses fail. What happens is this. The novice entrepreneur comes up with a great idea for a business, stocks up his shelves, opens his doors and then nothing happens. In our town I've seen so many examples of this, where would-be entrepreneurs arrive full of optimism that our town wants their gift shop, book shop, candle shop solely on the basis that we haven't already got one already.

Why haven't we got one of these shops? Is it maybe that no one either wants or needs whatever it is you're trying to sell them? Or if they do, perhaps there aren't enough potential customers to make the business viable. It's an easy mistake to make and I believe if you were to take a quick nationwide survey of everyone's garages, lock-ups, spare rooms and garden sheds, I bet you'd find thousands, probably millions, of products that were all part of that initial great idea, which ended in failure.

To succeed you must first identify your target market and understand their needs before you get your products and services together.

> Only when you have researched thoroughly, and decided that an actual market really does exist for whatever it is you're selling, should you actually go ahead with your business.

Not having a winning business plan is the other most common mistake made by would-be entrepreneurs.

If you go on an unfamiliar journey do you plan your route first, or wait until you're hopelessly lost before asking for directions?

I know a lot of you would say you wouldn't plan a route, and wait until either you got lost, got lucky or gave up.

But the point is you reach your destination faster and far less stressed if you invest a small amount of time preparing and familiarising yourself with the best route.

WHY BUSINESSES FAIL

There are many reasons why new businesses fail.

♦ Overestimating how much the business will sell or underestimating how long it will take to achieve initial essential sales targets.

♦ Underestimating costs.

♦ Failing to identify your market correctly because of inadequate market research, or no research.

♦ Failing to control costs.

- Carrying too much stock.

- Being personally and financially unprepared for running your own business.

Or in other words **failing to have a winning business plan**.

◆ EXPERIENCE ◆

When one of the shops in our small seaside town was up for let, I was intrigued to know who would rent it. In fact, I had thought about renting it myself and turning it into a cycle shop. However when I found out what rent the landlord wanted and the local council's business rates, I decided that it wasn't viable.

Personally I thought the rent was too high for our town. When I mentioned this to the letting agent they scoffed and dismissed my surmising as rubbish. Not only had they already had one offer, but were now turning down others.

The new tenant duly arrived and I watched with interest as what was once a tired sweet shop was transformed into a state-of-the-art Internet café.

I was shocked. Who in their right mind would consider opening an Internet café when the local council had just extended the library to include free Internet access for all library members? And those who weren't library members could pay a nominal fee of 50p to surf the web for 30 minutes.

Needless to say the new Internet café proprietor didn't appear to have any trade at all. Within weeks they closed only to reopen a few days later as a second-hand bookshop. Again surprising as there was already a large second-hand bookshop in what is a very small town.

Soon after the doors closed for good and the property went on the market again.

I don't take any pleasure telling you this story, but the reason it's important is that any one of us could end up in the same unfortunate position as that entrepreneur if all we do is follow our heart and go with the business idea that suits us most.

Unfortunately business doesn't work this way. Before you can even think about success, you need to be able to survive. There are two important words that I want to stress in the above list of reasons for business failures. They are:

◆ overestimating
◆ underestimating.

I speak from experience when I tell you that it's so easy to overestimate how much you will sell and underestimate how long it's going to take to get your business fully up and running.

I believe it can take at least three years to establish any worthwhile business. So prepare yourself for a long ride.

RESEARCHING YOUR IDEA

There are various areas of your idea that will have to be researched and looked at. The primary area that you need to concentrate on is to thoroughly research your product or service. Look at these from every possible angle.

Product or service

You need to be as sure as you can that either the product or service you are about to launch will actually appeal to your target market. Here's something to think about – why was the teabag a roaring success and the coffee bag a huge flop? I don't think anyone has actually managed to answer this one, but it does go to show that sometimes even though something similar has been an enormous success it doesn't mean that your new idea will work too. You can stack the odds in your favour by undertaking thorough research.

Question everything about your product or service and ask yourself:

◆ What makes your product/service unique?
◆ Why would customers choose you in favour of anyone else?
◆ How easily can you source your products?

In the initial burst of enthusiasm for your new business venture it's easy to overlook the question of sourcing. You need to be sure that not only you can obtain your products (or raw materials if making your own) but also that the price you're paying isn't subject to frequent and excessive price fluctuations.

◆ EXPERIENCE ◆

Our local fishmonger relied entirely on supplying his business from local fishing boats until recently. Although his unique selling point is to be able to sell fish so fresh it's often hopping and flipping all over his counter, the downside of this is that when the weather was too bad for the fishermen to fish, his business ran out of stock, which meant his customers began to buy elsewhere. To overcome this he now buys a percentage of his stock from fish wholesalers where he still manages to get fresh supplies for his business as well as offering locally caught fish when it's available.

The result has been an overall increase in his business as he has gained not only a reputation for always having fresh fish available, but also a greater variety than previously.

Currency fluctuations and transportation costs

If you're sourcing either products or raw materials from abroad you'll need to make sure that you allow provision somewhere in your costings for those inevitable currency fluctuations and other costs that can adversely affect the price you pay for your goods. Remember that the price that suppliers quote you when you're working out your initial costings may not be the price you actually have to pay when you open for business.

Another factor you'll need to consider is transportation costs, which can rise significantly in the event of an oil price increase, civil unrest or natural disaster.

I know an entrepreneur who sells sailing boats that he imports from France and Poland. He goes there himself and transports them back to the UK on a road trailer towed by his four-wheel drive. He believes this is the only way that he can ensure he gets his goods on time without paying excessive transportation costs and waiting weeks or even months for his boats to arrive.

Minimum quantity orders

Beware of the effect that having to order minimum quantities can have on your business.

We buy our Dutch bikes direct from Holland, which means we have to pay shipping costs. To keep costs to an absolute minimum our suppliers send our bike deliveries as fillers for other business trailers, so our bikes travel with all sorts of other goods such as fruit, flowers, vegetables and even cakes. The benefit to us is that we pay low transportation costs, but the disadvantages are that we have to order a minimum of 10 bikes to make up an order and our suppliers cannot give us an exact delivery date as our order is nothing more than a way of the haulage company ensuring they fill all the space in their trucks.

Another often unseen problem with minimum orders is you may not be able to order further stock as you haven't got the cash as all your money is already tied up in your stock.

This is why it's essential to work out a cash flow forecast.

Making your own products

You're intending to start a business where your unique selling point is that you make all your own products. How quickly can you make them? You'll need to be sure that you can keep making them while still running your business.

Whatever it is you're selling, make sure you can produce it as quickly as will be needed to make your business profitable. If you're marketing home-made produce, your customers will expect that's what they're getting. Offer anything else, and you may well destroy your uniqueness.

◆ **EXPERIENCE** ◆

A friend of mine makes the most beautiful dolls houses, together with a range of accessories.

Her attention to detail has gained her an enviable reputation both in the UK and abroad, with many of her products being purchased for the lucrative American market.

She was doing so well that she decided to move her business from exhibiting at craft fairs to taking on her own shop. However, soon after opening her shop she had to close it. Not because she couldn't find enough customers to support her expanding business, but because she couldn't make her products fast enough to keep up with demand.

Whereas before she spent her days working at her kitchen table crafting her products, she now had a shop to run, which meant she had little or no time left to make her products. Of course she could have hired someone to run the shop for her, but her business couldn't support employing staff as well as paying the hefty rent, business rates and all the other costs that come with a high street premises.

She's now back at her kitchen table doing what she loves most and her business is booming.

Packaging and promotion

Packaging and promotion of your goods often go hand in and. A product that is imaginatively and attractively packaged will obviously have greater a chance of being sold over one that is not. Toy manufacturers spend millions of pounds annually on making sure their products grab the attention of their intended audience, children.

Mail order

If you're intending to offer your products by mail order, you'll need to be sure:

◆ that your products are suitable for dispatch by either postage or by courier;

◆ they don't get damaged while in transit. You should also considering offering your customers insurance to protect their goods once they leave your business. You should also consider offering your customers insurance for their goods while being dispatched.

Selling at craft fairs and exhibitions
◆ Try to make all your customers walking advertisements by giving them something eye-catching to put their purchases in.

◆ Where possible choose packaging that has either been made from recycled materials or is capable of being recycled.

◆ Consider encouraging your clients to return their packaging to you for use again. You'll be surprised how many will do this and how many will buy from you because you offer this as a service.

Wholesaling your products
If you are selling your products wholesale you need to be sure that whatever you're selling remains in the same pristine condition once it reaches your customers' shelves as it did when it left you. Even though your clients are retailers and not the public, if your goods turned up damaged and unappealing few retailers will want to restock your orders.

Price

Unless you are proposing to sell a truly unique, sought-after product to a small niche market, consider very carefully the price at which you sell your goods and services before you throw open your doors.

 TIP ◆

If your prices are too low you may get the business, but not earn any money; too high and you won't sell anything.

The ethos that runs through all of the businesses that I am involved in is that we offer a value-for-money service where customer service is our number one priority. We're not bargain-basement clearance merchants. We offer a quality products at prices customers find attractive and leave enough profit to make it all worthwhile.

MARKET RESEARCH

Comparing like for like

When researching the competition, make sure that you are actually comparing like with like.

I recently came across an Internet business offering what appeared to be bicycles similar to the ones we sell. Naturally I was concerned that this business appeared to be offering considerably lower prices. However when I compared their cycles to ours it was apparent that they were not the same product in terms of specification and build quality.

Make a checklist

The best way to approach your research is to make a checklist of all the things you need to know about your competition before you start researching.

To be successful, research needs to be carried out over a period of time as opposed to on one occasion, as every business has seasonal peaks and troughs. Prices will vary depending on what time of the year it is. For example, most retailers suffer in the early part of the year when business is slow after Christmas. On the other hand this can be a boom period for gym owners and travel agents.

So make sure your research gives an accurate picture of the market in general and not one that is either enjoying a seasonal boom or a temporary famine!

How to find potential competitors

Obviously before you can start researching your competitors you must first identify who they are. The important point to remember is that it's not always the readily identifiable ones that you need to worry about.

Remember the poor guy who opened up an Internet café in my local town only to find that the local library were offering Internet access? These sorts of events aren't as uncommon as they might sound. Around about the same time as the Internet café disaster our local council opened a new restaurant, which they offered as a concession to a private company. The location of this restaurant is superb in that it gets the best views of the harbour. Naturally it's doing very well, but what about the private restaurant owners who are having to work doubly hard on the almost impossible job of winning customers back to their restaurants which have no sea views?

It's always a good idea to keep an eye on what your local council is up to. If nothing else you may well spot a business opportunity – a worthwhile concession up for tender.

The main ways to find your competitors is to check:

◆ advertisements in your hobbies' magazines, club websites and your local paper;

◆ the Internet – using the main search engines (Google, Yahoo!, etc);

◆ trade directories;

◆ *Yellow Pages*;

◆ *Thompson* directory.

Checking out the competition

When checking out the competition make sure you find out:

◆ Exactly what it is they are offering. How do their products or services compare to yours in terms of quality as well as price?

◆ The total price of their product once you've included all the extras. For example is VAT included or added on at the point of sale?

◆ The sort of guarantees your competitors are offering. Can you match or better what they are offering?

◆ How quickly they can deliver their goods. How does this compare to what you are offering?

◆ Customer testimonials. Have they included any customer testimonials in their sales material/website? If they have been established for any length of time they should have testimonials from satisfied clients. If they haven't, why not?

◆ How close they are to where you will be based. If they are on your doorstep is there really enough room for the two of you?

◆ How busy they are. If they have a retail business you should camp yourself discreetly outside at various different times to see how many people not just go into their shop, but also come out having made a purchase. If they are mail order or website based, monitor their site to see how often it is updated. Also send them some query emails to see how quickly they reply. It'll soon become apparent whether or not a business is doing well or dying on its feet.

Customer surveys

Sometimes the only reliable way to be sure that whatever it is you're about to sell is going to appeal to your potential market is to carry out customer surveys.

You can do this in a number of ways:

◆ If your hobby has a magazine with a readers' letters page, write to the editor with your idea asking for the readers' help with your research. Make sure you include your email address.

◆ Post messages on website discussion forum boards. Again, invite comments and suggestions regarding your proposal. This is a great way of getting some useful marketing feedback and if you encourage people to email their thoughts to you, you will then have a ready-made sales list for introducing your products or services.

◆ Send out questionnaires to clubs, groups and organisations relating to your hobby. Encourage participation by offering an incentive for everyone who completes them. For example, everyone who returns their questionnaire before such and such date will automatically be entered in our free prize draw to win a whatever it is you're offering.

◆ Network and mingle. Wherever your hobby enthusiasts gather, get out there and network with them. Most hobbies will have regular group get togethers, which can be great places to test drive any ideas you might have. For example, if you're introducing a new product or service you could go along and offer free test runs/trials for whatever it is you're offering. I use this technique a lot in my businesses when I'm planning to introduce something new. Not only have I found this a brilliant way of getting new ideas, but also for finding new customers.

Understanding the market place

Obviously it's unlikely that you will be the only business operating in your chosen field, but if you do find that the competition is thin on the ground this doesn't necessarily mean good news for your business. It may be that businesses like the one you are proposing have come and gone. So it's worth further research if there isn't any sign of real competitors.

Investigate as much as you can about your potential market. The following are good sources of market information.

♦ Internet search engines.
♦ Local libraries.
♦ Council records.
♦ Speaking to other shop owners who are operating in the geographical area you are considering.
♦ Newspaper archives.
♦ Posting 'information wanted' notices on web forums.
♦ Speaking to potential customers.

Prior to starting our cycle hire business, my partner and I spoke to as many of the local shop owners as we could, trying to find out whether or not they thought there was any future in our idea. Without exception everyone we spoke to was extremely helpful and offered us the benefit of their experience and came up with some useful suggestions.

So if you're planning to open a shop or business in a particular locality don't be afraid to ask existing businesses for their thoughts. That way you've got a good chance of finding out what's gone on in your area, and whether or not a business similar to what you're proposing has come and gone.

 TIP

I worry more about lack of competition than competition itself.

How much can I charge?

There's no easy answer to this one, and how much you sell will depend on a combination of factors including:

- how big your market is
- how well you promote your products and services
- your unique selling points
- your competitiveness.

The first thing you must get right is to actually ensure that there is a demand for whatever it is you are offering. Once you've established this you then need to be sure that there will be sufficient demand to make it profitable.

THE COST OF STARTING A BUSINESS

To succeed you will have to have a fairly accurate idea of how much it is going to cost to start your business.

A common mistake is to decide on the type of business you want to start and work backwards finding out, often too late, that you can't afford to keep going what you've already started.

 TIP

Make sure that you work out as accurately as you can how much it's going to cost you to start up.

When calculating your initial costs, you should consider:

- How much you will have to pay for your initial stock.

- Any specialist equipment or machinery that may be required.
- Vehicle costs.
- Registration or professional fees – for example you may need to employ a solicitor to read and report on a lease agreement, patent a product or pay local authority registration fees.
- Insurance costs.
- Costs of hiring additional storage space.
- Website costs.
- Stationery costs.
- Working capital.

Working capital

Working capital is the amount of money you have available to run your business on a day-to-day basis.

This is as opposed to fixed capital, which is the capital you use to buy your fixed assets, for example what you spend on items such as buildings, vehicles, machinery etc.

A common problem when it comes to working capital, and one that I've made in the past, is to underestimate how much working capital you actually need to keep your business up and running. For example, if your business involves selling a range of products you will always have money tied up in unsold stock. Not only that but when you sell your stock you will then need to buy additional stock to replace what you've sold. Thus even though your business will be receiving sales revenue (income from sales), you will have to reinvest some, or even all, of this revenue in purchasing replacement stock.

You'll also to have pay your ongoing business costs, which might include rent, business rates, heating, lighting, advertising and so on as well as paying yourself and any staff you may have.

You need either to have money available in the form of working capital, or access to a bank overdraft to cover your regular business expenses until such time as your business is fully able to support itself.

> **◆ TIP ◆**
>
> Always include a generous provision for working capital in your business plan.

Initially you might find that although you're busy, you are not earning very much, if indeed anything, because you're having to reinvest your revenue in your business.

It's a common problem and one you need to address at your business planning stage.

WHO IS GOING TO FINANCE YOUR NEW VENTURE?

There are a number of options available to you:

- use your own funds;
- bank loans;
- business angels;
- small firms loan guarantee.

Own funds

Wherever possible you should use your own funds. That way you won't be burdening your new business with loan repayments. Obviously this won't always be possible.

Bank loans

My experience of banks and their lending policies has been dismal to say the least – so much so that I don't think I will approach them again. Your ideas may be more successful than mine, but if you do get turned down for a loan don't take this to mean your ideas don't have any potential.

Business angels

This is my favourite funding option. Business angels are other successful entrepreneurs who, in return for a share in your business, will loan you money to start or expand your business. Obviously, you'll need to be satisfied that you can get on with your business angel and that you're happy to have someone else have a role in your business. The advantage of course is not only funding for your business but also the expertise these entrepreneurs can bring to your business.

You can find business angels by using the Internet and searching under key words: 'business angels', 'funding for business', 'venture capital' etc.

Small firms loans guarantee

The SFLG guarantees loans from banks and other financial institutions for small firms that have viable business proposals but have failed to get a conventional loan because of lack of security.

You can apply for a loan for sums of between £5,000 and £100,000, or if your business has been trading for more than two years you can apply for up to £250,000.

To be eligible you must be a UK company with an annual turnover of no more than £3m, or £5m if you are a manufacturer.

The SFLG guarantees 75 per cent of the loan. In return the borrower has to pay the Department of Trade and Industry a premium of 2 per cent on the outstanding amount of the loan.

You can get a loan for most business activities although there are some restrictions. Further information can be found on the DTI website at http://www.dti.gov.uk.

DEALING WITH SLOW AND NON-PAYERS

Hopefully you will have few instances where customers either refuse to pay you, or are slow in settling invoices.

When this happens you have a number of options, culminating in taking them to court. In my experience most customers will pay their bills before ever getting to the stage of having to threaten legal action. So it's important when dealing with an overdue account not to rush in wielding a sledge hammer when one isn't needed.

These are some things we do to encourage prompt payment in our business:

- Confirm our prices and what is included in a written estimate so customers know exactly how much they are going to have to pay. By doing this you reduce the likelihood of having a payment dispute at some later date.

- Do not routinely offer credit terms. We include in all our written estimates that our terms of business are that payment is made immediately upon completion of the job. When it comes to our retail cycle business, we only release the cycle when the bill has been paid, and not before.

We adopt the following procedures for dealing with late payers:

- Where a customer does not settle their bill immediately, we allow a period of no more than seven days for their cheque to arrive, after which time we send a polite reminder letter.

- If after a further seven days we still hear nothing, we phone our client and ask what the problem is. It's vital to keep dialogue friendly and non-threatening. There can be a number of genuine reasons why customers are late in paying.

- If after a further seven days we still haven't been paid, and there isn't a genuine reason why the bill hasn't been settled, we then write a final letter, sent by recorded delivery. It asks that payment in full is made by return, or if this is not possible, we are contacted immediately to advise when payment will be made. We also include in our letter that if we don't receive payment within seven days, we will reluctantly have to take out County Court Summons.

The County Court

Taking non-payers to the County Court should always be a last resort. Although the system is easy to use, it is far better to have your debt settled without the costs and time involved in preparing your case for court. You can if you wish employ a solicitor, however you will have to pay their costs upfront. If your application is successful in the courts you can reclaim your fees from the other side.

But be warned that even if the court makes a judgement in your favour, your delinquent customer might still not pay their account. Then you have to make a further application to the court to allow you recover the debt from them.

It can be a lengthy, tiring process, and you really must be sure the debt is great enough to be pursued.

You can get the all the information, forms etc you need to make a County Court Claim by visiting your County Court or their website at http://www.courtservice.gov.uk. Or you can phone the Business Debtline on 08001 976 026.

WRITING A WINNING BUSINESS PLAN

Most small business gurus (you know the types – the ones who've recently been made redundant having spent most of their corporate lives killing careers with PowerPoint presentations and now want to sell their perceived skills to small business entrepreneurs) will have us believe that the most important reason for having a business plan is so that we can borrow money for our businesses.

And their angle on this? To write one for us, for which of course we will have to pay them a fee.

Let's get one important thing clear about business plans – you don't need to have someone write one for you. I don't care if they've been Richard Branson's personal business planner for the past 20 years, the only person that can really write a truly winning business plan for your business is you.

Because these experts will never tell you that your idea is absolutely farcical and you'd be wasting your money. An expert's expertise is in writing business plans. So if the business you're planning to start is in anything other than business plans, the truth is that they probably know absolutely nothing about your business. But you do because it has something to do with your hobby. You know your hobby better than any paid expert whose real motivation for helping you will be his extortionate fees.

The 10 elements of a winning business plan

1. **A well-researched business idea** which includes information on what products and services you intend to offer, who your target customers are, details of your competitors and a general assessment of the market you are proposing to work in.

2. A clear idea of **how much it's going to cost** you to start your business.

3. A clear idea of **how long it is going to take your business** to become fully operational.

4. **A personal survival plan** detailing how you will survive during the initial period when your business is not actually earning you money, but costing you.

5. **A contingency plan** for what to do in the event that something unforeseen happens to either your business or you.

6. Details of **how you intend to fund your business** and, if you intend to borrow money, the plan should include details of those who you are hoping to borrow this money from together with anticipated repayment periods.

7. **Profit and loss forecast** where you work out how much your business is going to cost to run versus how much you're going to achieve through sales.

8. **Cash flow forecast**. Essential for every business because you work out how quickly and often you will receive cash into your business versus how much you will have to spend to continue trading.

9. **Operational details for your business,** which will include:
   - details of where your business will be based, including any additional business premises that you may need to rent (for example additional storage space for stock etc);
   - information on how many staff (if any) you will need to hire, where you intend to get these staff from and how much you're intending to pay them. (You should never rely on the goodwill of friends and relatives who offer to work for you for nothing. This is wholly unrealistic and if your business relies on others supplying their labour free of charge then you should be asking yourself if your business is really viable.)

10. **SWOT analysis** – what are the strengths, weaknesses, opportunities and threats facing your business?

Business plan format

If you're considering approaching a bank to help finance your business, your business plan will need to be presented in a certain format. In addition to the above information they'll want to know more about your career history including details of why you're suited to start and run this type of business. If you are in partnership with someone, or you are hiring specialist help, they'll want to know more about these key people before they are willing to lend you any money.

◆ **TIP** ◆

> Most banks now offer a very useful business planning software programme, which you can get free from your business banker. The business plan is laid out in template form and all you have to do is fill in the blanks.

Even if you're not planning to borrow any money, I'd recommend you take advantage of their free software as I've found the spreadsheets for calculating profit and loss to be invaluable. Having a system where you can change one item and then immediately see the effect on profit and loss figures saves enormous time working things out.

Presenting your business plan

The golden rule when presenting your business plan to prospective lenders is that you must be completely confident with the facts, figures and projections.

Your presentation should be:

- Clear and to the point: free of superfluous and distracting things such as jokes, anecdotes and over-familiarity.

- So well-rehearsed that it doesn't actually sound rehearsed.

- Convincing. Remember you're asking someone to invest money in your business, which means they are sharing in your risk. They need to be convinced you know what you're doing and that above all else you are confident that you can achieve what you are saying.

What to wear

Dress to impress, but make sure that whatever it is you choose to wear you feel comfortable and confident. Nothing is more soul-destroying than making a presentation to someone when you feel at a disadvantage because of the way you are dressed. Certainly if the business bankers that I've met in the past are anything to go by, traditional smart dress is essential as many are still trapped in some sort of unique time warp.

SUMMARY

1. The two most common and potentially disastrous mistakes made by novice entrepreneurs are to decide on a product or service and then try and find customers to buy from them and to start a business without a written business plan.

2. The advantage of working out a winning business plan is that you can identify and address potential problems before it's too late.

3. When researching your market make sure that you are comparing like for like when considering the competition. Even though two businesses may on the surface appear to be servicing the same market, they can be world's apart.

4. Try to get an accurate picture of your set-up costs before you start your business.

5. Don't forget working capital. Insufficient working capital is often a cause of many otherwise potentially good business ventures going under. Remember that in the early stages you will need to reinvest much of your initial earnings to build and develop your business.

5

Sales: The Beating Heart
of Your Business

SELLING – THERE REALLY IS NOTHING TO FEAR

Whatever business you're planning to start – be it to sell a product or offer a service, you're going to have to be able to sell, because if you are to survive and succeed your business will have to compete with other businesses. The only way to truly beat the competition isn't to undercut them or outdo them, it's to outsell them.

YOU DON'T HAVE TO BE A SALES EXPERT TO SELL

An expert is often described as 'someone from out of town carrying a briefcase'.

Nowhere is this truer when it comes to the perceived mystery and magic surrounding successful salespeople. All sorts of misconceptions abound with many people believing that if you haven't got the 'gift of the gab', or a 'killer instinct' then you won't possibly be able to sell anything.

The next time you have nightmares about having to do your own selling I want you to know that often selling is nothing more than you being able to ask potential customers one simple question. I'll tell you what that is in a minute, but first I want to explain what selling *isn't*.

Selling isn't about:
◆ talking your customers into buying something they don't want;
◆ selling them something at a grossly over-inflated price;
◆ developing a 'killer instinct', whatever that might be.

OK. That's what selling *isn't*. So what *is* selling?

> Selling is helping your customer buy what they want and then making sure that what they decide to buy, they buy from you.

Imagine you've just decided that you want to take up canoeing as a hobby. You're going to need a number of things to get you started, which might include finding a suitable training course, buying a new canoe, lifejacket, suitable clothing, books, videos, roof-rack etc.

You visit your local outdoor shop and once inside you're approached by a friendly and obviously knowledgeable salesperson who encourages you to have a good look around the shop without feeling under any obligation.

While you're busy browsing you overhear the sales staff answer others' questions and you're impressed with their knowledge. You also like the range of canoes in the shop but are a bit unsure about which ones might be suitable for you. So you approach the salesperson for some advice.

Now put yourself in the salesperson's shoes. Here you are with a shop full of canoeing goodies. You stock everything from books, videos and clothing to a wide range of canoes to suit a range of uses and budgets. And anything you haven't got in stock you can generally get in within 48 hours, or sooner depending on the item required.

You've just finished serving a regular customer when this person you have never seen in your shop before nervously approaches you asking for advice, which you freely give. Now you've got to make a choice – you can either smile at them as they walk out of the door on their way to search the Internet looking for a cheaper deal than you can offer, or you can be professional and sell them what they want.

Now if I was that salesperson, I'd want to sell them a canoe and all the bits and pieces they need. After all, I've given them the benefit of my advice, I know my products are quality and offer excellent value for money. Makes sense, doesn't it?

So why do so many otherwise competent salespeople allow their customers to walk out of the door of their shop without asking them one simple question?

What is the most powerful sales technique in the world?

Some salespeople will never grasp this, because it's so simple. The most powerful selling technique in the world is to *ask for the order*.

That's it. No expertise or killer instinct required. The most successful and simplest sales strategy that you can employ in your business is to say to someone, 'Would you like to buy it?'

Of course there are lots of different ways you can ask potential customers to buy whatever it is you're selling, but the question remains the same.

Selling has nothing to do with foot-in-the-door techniques or pushiness. We all know that these so called sales techniques are used by all sorts of individuals and corporations on a daily basis. But the reason for this is because they can only sell whatever it is because either nobody wants it, or it is grossly over-priced.

You won't have to employ any of these unscrupulous tactics because as a Kitchen Table Entrepreneur you're going to be offering quality, value-for-money goods or services to people who really need them.

So you have nothing to fear!

Remember that people like to buy things. The only thing that is worse than a morose, unhelpful salesperson is one that leaves you to 'think' about things.

THE THREE GOLDEN RULES FOR SELLING ANYTHING TO ANYONE

1. Remember that people buy *benefits* not features.
2. You must give your customers a reason for buying from you – otherwise they'll buy from someone else.
3. If you're doubtful about selling whatever it is you're selling, people will be afraid to buy it.

Rule 1. People buy benefits not features

Believed to be the first rule in marketing, the 'people buy benefits not features' mantra is at the heart of every advertisement you're ever likely to come across.

To sell anything to anyone you must understand this concept and appreciate that if you're adhering to this rule in your face-to-face sales presentation, brochures or website information, the chances of your sales being anything less than average are greatly reduced.

Why is this concept so important? To answer this we need to look at the reasons we buy anything. Factors that influence what we buy include things like:

♦ price;
♦ what we need the whatever we're buying for;
♦ attractiveness – is it 'us'?

Price
Of course there can be an infinite amount of reasons why we might buy anything, but unless we've unlimited resources price will certainly be a deciding factor.

Marketing companies are aware of this, and many competing products highlight price as being a benefit.

Next time you hear a radio commercial, watch a TV advertisement or pick up a magazine, start looking for the benefit messages. What's in it for you? What will you get if you buy a certain product? Will you feel better? Slimmer? Fitter? Wealthier? Sexier? Younger?

Selling is all about benefits

The reality is that we don't buy things because of features, we buy because of the benefits that come with owning a certain product or service.

One of my businesses is running a gardening maintenance company. Many of my clients lead busy professional lives, which means that they are 'time poor'.

All of them want to enjoy a nice relaxing garden to unwind in, without having to spend all of their free time cutting lawns, weeding borders, trimming hedges and so on.

So the features of the service my business offers are that we undertake all aspects of garden maintenance, including lawn cutting, hedge cutting, pruning etc.

But the benefits to our clients are that they enjoy more free time in their wonderful garden because they no longer have to spend hours maintaining it.

When we market our service we list our features (what we offer), but we sell our benefits. Therefore in our business our advertisements are always built around powerful *benefit* messages.

> Tired of spending all your free time mowing the lawn, cutting hedges and travelling to and from your local dump?
>
> Here at Paul Power Landscapes we're experts at doing the things you hate.
>
> Isn't it time you enjoyed your free time and your garden?

The features are:
◆ lawn cutting
◆ hedge cutting
◆ dumping of garden waste.

The benefits are:
◆ enjoyment
◆ free time.

Putting your sales message together

The way to construct your sales message is to highlight the features first, followed by all the benefits.

Start looking at as many advertisements as you can. The glossy magazines that come with weekend newspapers are very useful as they usually contain lot of imaginative ads often with the 'benefit message' innovatively hidden somewhere within the message.

We can learn lots from looking at how other businesses market their products.

Get into the habit of either cutting out advertisements and keeping them in a file, or writing down the advertising message and keeping it in your notebook. Then when the time comes to write your own ads you can browse through your file for inspiration.

Don't forget that the feature/benefit rule also applies to face-to-face selling. Next time you're out shopping listen to what salespeople are telling potential customers.

Ignore the completely inept ones, usually hired by larger DIY stores and electronic warehouse retailers, but wait until you find real salespeople. You will hear the same message: 'But the great thing about this is that it ...' – and you'll hear the *benefit* loud and clear. The more skilled the salesperson the more suited the benefit will be.

But not everyone buys the same benefit!

We all have different reasons for buying anything. Take, for example, someone buying a flight ticket. Unless it's a holiday charter airline the people buying a seat on a flight will have different needs.

Some will be travelling on business, others holidaying and others wanting to travel as cheaply as possibly.

To overcome the problem of differing needs, airlines target their marketing campaigns at different sectors. Comfort and getting you there on time will be key benefits for business travellers, while value for money might be the message for holidaymakers.

In your business it may not always be possible, owing to budget restrictions, to target different market sectors, so make sure the benefits you're selling appeal to the widest audience possible.

> ◆ TIP ◆
>
> If you're face-to-face selling then all you have to do is to correctly identify the buyer's needs and sell them a benefit that they want.

If they need whatever it is you're selling right now, and you have it in stock, then the obvious benefit is that they can have it now. Wait and think about it and it may be gone.

If they're working to a budget and whatever it is they want comes within it, the benefit is that not only can they have it, but they can save themselves money by not spending all their budget.

Look at what you're proposing to sell

Whatever it is you're planning to sell, start by listing all its features and then work on the benefits.

Be imaginative here. Many of the benefits may not be immediately apparent to you even though it's your product or service.

Start by trying to see whatever it is you are selling from different perspectives:

- Is it only suitable for everyone who shares your hobby, or could it be of use to a wider market?

- How does it compare with other like goods or services in terms of price and quality?

- How quickly can you deliver?

- Can you give five reasons why anyone should buy your product/service instead of your competitors'?

- If your product/service has no competitors, why? Some of your reasons should make excellent benefits.

Once you've come up with your list of benefits you're almost ready to sell anything to anyone, but you must learn and follow the remaining two golden rules of selling.

Rule 2: You must give your customers a reason to buy from you

Ideally you should give your customers as many reasons as you possibly can for buying from you, although often this isn't possible. But the bottom line still remains – if you don't give a good enough reason, people will buy elsewhere.

I want you to think about something you need to buy. This could be anything – an essential item, luxury treat or something you buy everyday like a newspaper or carton of milk.

Now on a blank piece of paper write down the item you've just thought of and draw a big circle around it.

Immediately underneath your circled item write down where you intend to buy this item and draw a circle around it. Don't give this too much thought; just write down where you'd first go to buy it.

Done?

Now draw a line from the item and then draw another big circle. In this circle write down all the places you could actually buy this item. Write down as many places as you can think of, stopping only when there is no more space left in your circle. (If you can't think of any alternative places to buy from then choose another item and start the exercise again.)

Finally, draw a line and another big circle from the circle where you've written where you're planning to buy this item. Then write in it as many reasons as you can think of why you've decided to buy from this source.

Your findings

This exercise is to show you that although you made an initial choice where to buy your item, there are other places you could buy it.

In business, these other outlets are called competitors, and to survive and compete with our competitors we must be able to offer would-be customers a reason to buy from us.

Why did you make that initial choice? Cost? Location? Or something else? Marketers often refer to these reasons as a business's **Unique Selling Points** (USPs).

What are your business's Unique Selling Points?

To do this, break down your product/service into set categories:

◆ price
◆ quality

- availability
- uniqueness.

Price

Unless you intend building an out-of-town pile-'em-high sell-'em-cheap style warehouse, it's unlikely that you will want to sell on price alone. However, price will still be a deciding factor for potential customers. For example if you're planning on running your business as a mail order shop, your goods will need to be keenly priced to get customers buying from you. The USP for mail order businesses is often that they offer goods cheaper than anyone else.

On the other hand, if your business will involve lots of personal attention and fussing over your clients' every wish, your prices will be higher than your competitor offering a bargain basement, no-frills service.

In this case your USP could be that you are expensive, but well worth it because you are offering personal service.

Quality

What makes your goods and services better than anyone else's?

It's not enough to simply say the word 'quality'. Your USP needs to paint a picture. Bed manufacturers are a good example of this. We all know that the difference between a good and bad night's sleep can be the quality of the bed, so a cheap bed may mean a bad night's sleep. Buyers will therefore spend more on a bed that promises restful sleep.

Again it's not enough simply to promise a restful night's sleep, as most of the beds in the shop will be claiming the same thing. The unique selling point will often be to highlight how many springs or layers this bed has over its competitors.

Availability

Ignore this one at your peril.

We're living in a world where the words 'next week' often lose a sale. Even next-day delivery can be too late for some people, so if your product is available to be bought and taken home today, it is a Unique Selling Point.

For example I've now given up furniture shopping in chain stores for the simple reason that no matter how small the item, even a chair, it has to be ordered by the sales staff. Even though you have paid for the item you have no idea of when it's likely to arrive. Finally, after what seems like an extraordinarily long wait you get a phone call to say the furniture will arrive 'sometime on Friday'. When you explain you'll be at work on Friday and need a specific time so you can arrange for someone to be there, you're told this isn't possible.

I'm not alone in switching my allegiance back to the small independent retailer who either has the item already in stock or will personally get it in for you and deliver it to you at a mutually convenient time. Availability is always a powerful unique selling point.

Uniqueness

Many businesses based around a hobby are successful because what they are offering is unique.

Large retailers, travel companies and the like steer clear of what is often referred to as niche markets. The last thing they want is a large amount of their store shelf space clogged up by products that relatively few customers will be interested in.

Therefore your unique selling point could be that you're offering hard-to-find items such as books, memorabilia or even specialist holidays.

 ◆ TIP ◆

Highlight whatever makes your business unique as a selling point. It can even be something as simple as your personal knowledge of what you sell.

◆ EXPERIENCE ◆

A few years ago the rudder on my sailing boat broke in half while we were in heavy seas. Although the boat was fibreglass, the rudder was wooden. I searched everywhere to find a replacement rudder with no avail. Even desperate surfing on the Internet brought no results.

Finally, on the advice of a friend, I spent a morning walking around what I'd previously thought were disused warehouses. Here amongst the carcasses of forgotten old boats, I found John's workshop. As soon as I met him I knew he was skilled and competent. Not because of anything he said. It was everything about him. The way he lovingly handled his measuring tape, the way he examined my broken rudder – everything about him told me he loved what he was doing. He had the KTE passion.

My instincts were right and a couple of weeks later my new rudder was ready, but when I went to collect it he had bad news. He told me he was sorry that he was going to have to charge me so much, but he'd put a lot of work into it and it was made from mahogany.

The rudder was a work of art. He handed it to me lovingly wiping it down with a cloth to remove his hand prints from it.

'How much?' I asked expecting to pay at least £150. He apologised again. '£20,' he said.

I was shocked. So much so that it was obvious on my face. Unfortunately he took it to mean I was shocked at the price and began to justify his costs again.

After convincing him that not only was I very pleased with the new rudder but also believed he was grossly under-pricing his work, he told me that no one wanted wood any more. 'Everyone wants fibreglass now,' he said, 'wood is just too high maintenance.'

When I next passed John's workshop the doors were shut and soon after the whole area was redeveloped for luxury housing.

Clearly John's USP was that he was a skilled craftsman and experienced boat builder. Since meeting John I have spoken to many people who would give almost anything for his skill and experience. While the new boat market is dominated by no-maintenance fibreglass crafts, there are still a large number of sailors who prefer wooden boats, and some would say there has been a high revival in wooden boats in recent years.

It's difficult to say why John failed to see that his USP was his uniqueness, but I do think that probably one of the reasons why he decided to close his business was that he wasn't earning enough. Certainly if his prices were anything to go by he was seriously undercharging, and these super-low prices could only be sustained for so long.

Was John trying to compete on price with the plastic boat builders? I don't know, but what I can say is that it does look like he failed to correctly identify his USP.

Having something unique to offer is a great selling point. Our lives are dominated by mass-produced, over-priced garbage. We'd give almost anything to be able to get our hands on something different.

What makes your future business different from others is that you are going to be working at something you really enjoy doing. The enthusiasm and passion you bring to your products and services is what makes your business as unique and special as you are.

◆ TIP ◆
Never undersell yourself.

Rule 3. Don't be doubtful about what it is you're selling

One of the reasons that many otherwise professional salespeople fail to reach sales targets is that they don't really believe in what they're selling. It is often the problem when you work for someone else where the sales department has little control over the quality of the products or service they're selling.

This is the problem with the large furniture stores I mentioned previously. My experiences have been that you walk in and are pounced on by an over-zealous salesperson who follows you around the store like a puppy saying how wonderful and nice everything that you look at is.

As soon as you say something negative about a piece of furniture they agree with you and do their best to move you on to the next equally unimaginatively piece in the hope that you will say yes. And all throughout you're subjected to the information that there's 50 per cent off this weekend, and that the now mandatory interest-free credit is available on that particular item.

Text-book sales stuff. The salesperson sells you the benefits (as they see them) – interest free credit, etc. And of course somewhere along the line they will get in their unique selling point, which could be something like, 'Of course this suite is part of our super-duper executive range and is exclusive to us,' and just in case your comprehension of the English language is as bad as they assume your financial position to be, they'll add 'which means you can't get it anywhere else.'

However, where it all falls apart is when you test the confidence they have in their product.

Some good questions to ask are:

- Who makes the furniture?
- Where is it made?
- When can you deliver it? Get specific here – 'when' as in morning? Afternoon? Mid-afternoon?
- Has anyone ever cancelled an order with your store?
- What happens if my furniture is late – will you phone me, or someone from your call centre?

If the store prides itself on its reputation for customer service, and consequently has little or no problems, then this will quickly become apparent from the salesperson's response.

However if they don't have such good customer service, the cracks will soon start to appear. Don't be surprised when the salesperson decides to leave you alone to 'think about it' while they go and badger someone else.

The problem is that they're not confident in their product. They've been at the store too long now to know that many of their orders won't be delivered on time, and that there can be a whole range of other problems, such as the wrong product being delivered or an incorrect colour suite.

Unless you're a seasoned conman, you won't be able to sell unless you believe in what you're selling.

Before starting your business make sure you have confidence and faith in what you're about to start. There's often a temptation to cut corners and decide that whatever you're selling will be 'all right on the night' sort of thing.

Trust me – it won't. Kitchen Table Businesses succeed because their owners believe completely in what they're offering. Their enthusiasm and passion sells and builds their businesses.

Special offers, interest-free credit and free delivery are the domain of the stack-them-high sell-them-cheap brigade. Our businesses are different. You are different. Go out and create something unique and wonderful and you won't need any costly, frilly incentives to get customers queuing at your doors.

OVERCOMING OBJECTIONS

The most notable difference between giving something away and selling it, is objections.

If you've already set up your business and you find you're not at least on occasions getting objections from potential customers then it probably means you're giving it away! Because customer objections are a natural part of the *buying* process, not the *selling* process.

Unfortunately many sellers misinterpret an objection as being a reason someone doesn't want to buy, when in fact it is a clear buying signal.

As soon as the 'but's, and 'what if's start flowing, the inexperienced salesperson incorrectly assumes that what they thought was a potential buyer isn't one after all. Consequently the seller's shutters go down, the wrong message is given out to the would-be buyer, and in an instant any chance of a sale is lost.

◆ TIP ◆

An objection is a clear buying signal.

If you're to successfully overcome customer objections you must understand that they're actually not objections at all. They are buying questions, or buying signals.

Imagine for a moment someone is planning a holiday to some far-flung exotic destination. Somewhere they have never been before. They know roughly the area where they want to go to because friends went there some time ago and said they really enjoyed it.

So they go off to the local high street travel agent. They could search the Internet, but they really want to talk to someone about this holiday because although their friends told them it was lovely, and they saw the breath-taking holiday pictures, others have since said that the area is dangerous and holidaymakers can be at risk from local criminal gangs.

You are the travel agent. You are very helpful and pull out all the brochures on the areas. When you run through some of the prices they're a little taken aback because their friends didn't pay this much. So they tell you that it sounds a bit expensive, and isn't really what they were hoping to pay.

Expensive, is the first objection.

Now you have two options:

1. Decide to stop wasting their time and politely invite them to browse through the brochures when they get home while you get on with the next customer.

2. Overcome the objection, or, if this is not possible, interest them in an alternative holiday that fits their budget.

If you are a more inexperienced salesperson you are more likely to opt for number one. On the other hand if you are more experienced you will know from experience and hopefully training that saying it's too expensive means that the customer is interested in buying the holiday.

Why?

Well let's look at the obvious first. You're sitting in your high street shop and they walk in asking about a holiday to a specific destination. In anyone's mind that should be seen as a fairly strong buying signal.

When you start telling them how much it's likely to cost they indicate that sounds a bit expensive and is more than they were hoping to pay. Again this is a positive buying signal. They haven't said, 'I don't want to go there,' all they've said is that it's more than they were hoping to pay.

So what you need to do now is to overcome their objection. The easiest way of doing this is with some gentle questions, beginning with, 'I'm sorry to hear that because obviously you're very keen on going there. Well let's not give up yet and see what we can do for you.'

You've told your customer two important things. First that you're sorry it sounds expensive, and second that you are going to help them get the holiday they want.

Before going any further you need to know:

◆ Is it too expensive because the customer can't afford it?
◆ Have they found a cheaper deal elsewhere?
◆ It is just more than they thought it would cost?

You can ask anyone anything you want without them getting offended, provided you're polite about it. So you ask them: 'When you say it's more than you expected to pay is that because you're seen a cheaper deal elsewhere?'

Notice I used the word 'cheaper'. I could have said 'better', but that would have been commercial suicide because what I've told my potential customer is that somewhere out there, there is a better deal to be had.

◆ TIP ◆

Always use 'cheaper' and not 'better' when dealing with a price comparison.

Cheaper doesn't mean better, it usually means inferior, so when you're in this sort of situation choose your words carefully.

Your customer now tells you the full story. 'Well the reason it's more than I expected is because my friends went there and they paid a lot less.'

Because you know your business you will know why there is a price difference. There may be a number of reasons why it's more expensive now and you might even find their friends' holiday company isn't around any more having gone bankrupt.

Now you're ready to overcome the objection.

Because you've probed a bit more into the reason your customer believes it may be too expensive you're in a better position to overcome their objection. But before you do that you need to know whether or not the holiday is within your customer's budget. You do this by asking, 'How much are you planning to spend on your holiday?'

Some salespeople will disagree with me when I tell them this saying that you're going to insult your customer. However, in all the years I've been running my own businesses no one has been insulted by this question. In fact quite the opposite has happened and they've been pleased to be able to give me something that I can work on to come up with a package to suit their needs.

Provided the holiday is within your customer's budget then there is no reason why they shouldn't want to book their holiday with you. Unless of course there are more objections!

Which in this case we know there will be, because our customer has heard some negative things about others who have gone to this area.

But of course in your position as salesperson you don't know this and just as you thought you'd got the order, your efforts are under attack again when you're told, 'I don't know how true it is but I've heard that a number of tourists have been robbed when they go to this area...'

Fear of being robbed is now your second objection.

Provided the area isn't marred by frequent robberies you'll be able to allay your customer's fears. Obviously honesty is the best policy and you do have a legal duty of care to your customers, which includes not misleading them.

How to turn objections into immediate sales

As we've seen, objections are really buying signals because the buyer is really asking questions that, if answered favourably, will mean they can buy whatever is being sold.

Certain types of objections, if handled the right way, can be turned into immediate sales. In a few moments we'll look at different ways of closing a sale. Often objections offer the easiest way of closing a sale so that everyone is happy; what's often referred to as win-win situation.

◆ TIP ◆

A win-win situation is where the buyer gets what he wants at a price the seller is happy to sell at.

The price objection

One of the most common objections you're likely to encounter is the customer who tells you you're too expensive. Often buyers use this objection hoping to get a better deal. You can use this strategy to your advantage by leaving a degree of negotiation in your pricing structure.

I say 'degree' as the last thing you want to do is get a reputation for having prices that are always negotiable. That said, I don't think there's any harm in having a small negotiating margin where your overall profits won't suffer if you agree somewhere below your original asking price.

This is how it works. You give absolutely nothing away unless you get the sale there and then. No more buts, ifs, I'll think about its. Simply, 'If I agree will you buy it right now?'

If your buyer says no, he won't or can't, then there's no deal and it remains fixed at its original price. However if he does agree to buy now he gets the item at a reduced price.

The power of silence

Silence is a much underestimated selling technique. Too often salespeople rush in and spoil a sale because they just can't stay silent for long enough. Unfortunately many of us are programmed to find silence unbearable, but silence is a natural part of the buying process.

Think of the last time that you either made a significant purchase or bought something you wouldn't usually buy. Chances are that you didn't simply waltz into the shops, see the item, holiday, house, service and immediately buy it. Like most of us you'll have needed some time, even if only a few seconds, to think it through.

During this thinking time you say nothing. Your mind is on what you're about to do and any sort of conversation can at best be an extremely annoying interruption and at worst make up your mind that you don't want whatever it is after all.

♦ TIP ♦

Silence is a powerful selling technique.

It's also something that takes a bit of getting used to because most of us find silences uncomfortable. Therefore rather than wait until you're at that crucial moment where everything depends on your staying quiet long enough to win the sale, start practising now.

A good way to do this is to start using the silent technique next time you're buying something. You'll be amazed at how quickly prices come down when you simply say nothing.

The most effective places to try this technique are at large retail chain stores where the salesperson's income rely heavily on them closing sales. Although many of these outfits have perpetual sales and give-away offers this doesn't mean there isn't room for further negotiation.

The technique works as follows:

1. Make yourself known to someone from the sales staff.

2. Discuss your requirements.

3. Even if the price is displayed, ask how much it costs.

4. When the salesperson tells you the price, say absolutely nothing. Instead keep staring at the item.

5. Wait.

6. Do not say anything. Savour the silence while the salesperson starts to shift uncomfortably. If they're working on a commission the chances are the first thing they tell you is that the price could be reduced...

Trust me, this technique works, which is why when you're selling something you must out-silence your buyers.

Although silences can last an agonising amount of time, it will actually only be a matter of seconds. A minute at the most and during that time your buyer will be thinking about what they're about to do, not trying to outwit you.

Being mentally prepared is important. Remember, as soon as you give your price, *shut up*. Say nothing until your buyer speaks.

And when they say 'I'll take it,' you know it's all down to the power of silence.

CLOSING TECHNIQUES

The technique of turning a buyer's interest into a sale is known as closing a sale.

Depending on which book you read you will find a bewildering choice of techniques to choose from. However, I believe you only need to concentrate on three. We've already covered the most important one

Ask for the order
In my experience this is often the most appropriate and easiest method of getting the sale.

It's amazing how often sales staff don't do this. Instead they talk on and on and round and round, desperate to do anything but actually ask for the order. Then wonder why the customer buys somewhere else.

So always ask for the order. Even if the customer doesn't appear too interested in what you're selling – still ask for the order. And if they say no, ask them why. After all, you've invested your time in showing them whatever it is you're selling, so it makes sense to know why they now don't want it.

The assumptive close
My second favourite method is to simply assume your customer is going to buy from you. The secret to using this method is to start planting the seeds of success right from the beginning.

When I meet a prospective client for my landscape gardening business, I always include lines like this somewhere during the meeting:

'When we come and do your garden would it be all right if we parked on your driveway?'

'Do you have an outside tap that we could use?'

'Generally we like to get onsite everyday at about 8am. That wouldn't be too early, would it?'

'Would you like me to arrange for you to see examples of some of our work?'

Not only am I assuming that I will be getting the order, but I'm also asking questions. I always ask the last question as this shows my prospective client that I'm confident enough to be able to show them examples of our company's work. I don't wait for them to ask me.

Questions like these help build up a rapport with your client and also establish you as a professional. Few cowboys will give a stuff about what time they get to their customers' gardens, and most will never want anyone to see examples of their work.

You can use the assumptive closing technique for any business. All you have to do is work out some appropriate questions and introduce them into your discussions at appropriate intervals.

Try and avoid using sentences like: 'If we're lucky enough to get your order,' or, 'If we can agree a price,' and so on. Sentences like these create doubt. They are based on 'if's and also give the impression that your price is in some way negotiable.

◆ TIP ◆

Be positive in your assumptions.

Generous use of the word *when* will pay dividends. *When* we come, *when* you book with us, *when* your order arrives, *when* you decide which colour, *when* you stay with us, etc.

Remember that very often people 'buy' people. This is especially true of many businesses based on hobbies.

For example, if someone is planning to go on a painting holiday they're going to have to be certain they like who'll be teaching the course. These are people businesses where those attending want more than just a painting course. They want to enjoy the whole experience.

The assumptive close has always worked for me and I think it takes a lot of the fear out of selling. One of the advantages is that there's no big build up to a grand finale where suddenly you must close the sale.

Relax and assume they'll be your customers and most likely they will.

The alternative close

Another powerful closing technique is to use is what's often referred to as the 'alternative closing method'.

The idea here is that rather than offer your customer the choice between buying and not buying, you include an alternative. So the decision is now *what* to buy, as opposed to *will* I buy?

It's an effective technique that's easy to introduce. In its basic form all you need to do is offer a choice. So if someone is browsing your hand-crafted, keep-out-all-draughts knitted sweaters, then all you need to do is introduce a choice, which could be a different colour or size. Then ask your customer which one would they prefer. 'Would you like the black one or the grey one?' 'Small or large?'

You're using two closing techniques here. Assumptive and alternative. So you're assuming your customer will buy one – but which one. You're not being pushy here, just helpful. After all how many of us have walked out of shops because they didn't have the size or the colour we wanted and were either too shy, too busy or whatever to bother asking.

But imagine you've offered an alternative colour and your customer says no to both. What then? Ask them what they're looking for. The important thing here is to keep the dialogue going. Keep them interested and stop them from going elsewhere.

Remember that lots of people browsing your goodies may not be buying for themselves. They could be looking for gifts for someone else. By asking them what they're looking for and who it's for you'll get a better understanding of their needs and be better placed to help them and close your sale.

So the alternative close can go on until they either buy something, or you run out of alternatives. Provided you don't come across as pushy or stalk them! Remember you're there to help them find the thing they most want to buy.

Price alternatives are good, too.

Let's say that your business involves you selling home-made soaps. Because your product is unique and all of your scented, bubbly delights are lovingly created, they're considerably more expensive than traditional off-the-shelf soaps.

Limiting yourself to one price range can lead to problems and you could find, as many gift shops do, that your shop is full of 'Sunday browsers' oohing and cooing over everything, but buying nothing. The problem here is often that the prices are just out of reach of the average impulse purchaser.

The way to address this is to offer two price ranges. One that appeals to those who appreciate the quality and uniqueness of your soap and will buy it whatever the cost, and one for those who would love to buy your soap if it was more affordable.

If you're creating your own products then you could offer a certain product range at a reduced price to the second group. Or have a special offer bucket where you include all your soaps that haven't come up to the same exacting standards as the others.

Whatever you do, try to offer alternative prices. If someone looks interested but then disappointed when they see the price of your soap and makes for the door, get in there. Tell them you do a special range of soaps which are excellent value and bring out your irresistible soaps with a more appealing price tag.

We all like choice. Whether it's choice within a product range or choice of prices, we're more likely to buy when we don't feel as if we're simply buying the first thing we've seen.

MASTER THE THREE PS OF SELLING

Undoubtedly, closing techniques are important. Nothing is worse than seeing a potential customer buy from the competition when they've already been discussing their requirements with you.

That said, there's much more to selling than just closing techniques. What happens along the road to agreeing the sale is often where any chance of a sale is lost. If you pay enough attention to the three Ps then many of your sales will close by themselves.

The three Ps are:

1. Prospecting
2. Presentation
3. Price.

Prospecting

Selling is one thing that you can't leave to luck. Few, if any, businesses have ever succeeded, let alone survived, because they got lucky. Successful entrepreneurs make their own luck by getting out there and preparing the ground for future success. Great sales figures don't just happen. It's a combination of making sure the product is right for the market we're selling in.

◆ EXPERIENCE ◆

A few years ago I wandered around Brighton market hoping to find some old vinyl records on behalf of a friend. After a short time browsing the stalls I found what I was looking for, a stand specialising in records, posters and memorabilia.

You could say I got lucky. How many markets, boot fairs and the like would have someone selling records? But there was nothing lucky about it. I must confess I'm not a fan of boot fairs and the thoughts of having to spend a Saturday or Sunday morning wandering round a wet field with the waft of sausages and onions doesn't do it for me.

Careful not to either waste my time, or make myself miserable in the process, I asked everyone I knew where would be the best place to pick up vinyl records and they all pointed me in the direction of this particular market. So my success was really down to spending a little time preparing and planning.

While I was there I took the opportunity of browsing the stalls. To my amazement many were full of all sorts of interesting things and ideas and these businesses were doing a brisk trade.

However other businesses weren't. It wasn't difficult to see why. The people who were browsing in the market were either looking for something unique and interesting, or something regular but at a much cheaper price than they would expect to pay in a high street shop.

Therefore the businesses that were doing well had matched their products to the people who visited the market, and the traders that weren't doing well clearly hadn't thought about the type of market they were selling to.

A bit like selling football stripes at a chess conference.

Presentation

One of the most powerful selling techniques I know is simply to present both yourself and your product with the utmost respect, which means dressing appropriately and packaging your product correctly.

Dressing well

When I meet a prospective client for the first time I dress appropriately. Although most people say they wouldn't mind their landscape gardener turning up covered in mud, sweat and cement, often they do. And even if they wouldn't be put off, I still wouldn't turn up looking like this – because it would put me off.

Dressing to impress is important. If your appearance is dirty and sloppy people will expect whatever you're selling to be the same. Similarly if you handle your product as if it is a piece of rubbish you immediately devalue it.

Whenever I give anyone my business card I hand it to them as if I were giving them a precious gem. I do this because I know that our business delivers a quality, value-for-money service, something all too rare these days.

If you're going to slap a dog-eared, ink-splurged home-produced card in a prospective client's hand you may as well be giving them your competitor's phone number.

Displaying your product

Next time you're out for a Sunday afternoon stroll, take a closer look at why you want to spend time looking in some windows and not in others. It's all to do with presentation. Most antique shops have retail display down to a fine art, as do successful florists. It's all about display. Even the most mundane product can be made to look appealing in the right window.

Whether you sell at craft fairs, exhibitions, boot fairs, church halls or with an online shop, presentation is the key to success. Get that right and you will at least have customers coming through your doors or stopping at your stand. Get it wrong and everyone loses out.

Creating atmosphere

Often the difficulty with a small shop is creating the right atmosphere. A small, silent shop can be as intimidating as a large austere public building. Make it easier for potential clients to browse your wares. Invite them in with the sound of relaxing music and heavenly scents.

Inviting people in

Display a notice on your door. Something like, 'Please do come in and browse – you're under no obligation whatsoever to buy anything.'

And then once they are inside, make your visitors feel at home. Be warm and friendly but not in an overpowering way. Have some music playing in the background as this helps take away that church-like silence you often get in smaller shops.

Remember to offer them alternatives. 'Too big.' 'We've got smaller ones as well.' 'Too expensive.' 'We do have some on special offer.'

'Not really me.' 'What is you?'

'Can't make up my mind?' 'Why not have them both?'

Listen to what your visitors are saying without intruding on their viewings and then at the right moment offer them the alternatives.

And at all times avoid that awful, insincere greeting: 'How can I help you?' To which I'm always tempted to reply, 'You could pay this month's mortgage...'

 TIP

People like buying things, especially something that they'll be using for their favourite hobby. So make it easy for them to buy.

Price

Whatever you're selling it must be priced to appeal to your target market.

Too expensive and you won't sell any, too cheap and you won't earn enough profit to stay in business long enough to repay your initial financial investment.

From now on start becoming price aware. Whenever you see products or services that you're thinking of offering in your business, stop and really look at what price they are being sold at.

Ask yourself: Can you sell them any cheaper?

If your products will retail for more, ask yourself why should anyone choose what you're offering over a cheaper alternative?

Many products, even so called hand-crafted products, are mass produced in sweatshops in developing countries. You face an impossible task competing with these businesses who can retail goods and earn a profit for far less than it would probably cost you to buy these goods wholesale. While no business should compete on price alone, your prices still have to be attractive in order to sell your goods.

Record your price findings in a notebook along with details of potential suppliers, wholesalers, packaging companies etc. All useful information when it comes to finalising your plans.

FIVE WAYS TO TURBO-BOOST YOUR SALES

My top five recommendations for turbo-boosting your sales:

1. Accept credit and debit cards.
2. Include a mail order facility.
3. Offer customer referral incentives.
4. Publish your own newsletter.
5. Send a card.

Accept credit and debit cards

Even if you don't have a shop you should still consider taking credit and debit cards, especially if you sell at craft fairs, exhibitions and so on, and what you sell is of relatively high value.

Let's say you're selling bespoke bird boxes with every imaginable treat for bird and buyer, and the price starts at £30. Not a huge amount by any means but how many of us have £30 in our wallets?

◆ EXPERIENCE ◆

A local photographer did some brochure work for me recently and told me that if it weren't for him accepting cards his business would have closed years ago. The chances of anyone having as much as £20 in their wallets these days was about as likely as snow in August.

Even though expensive, it's worth it. Obviously you'll have to shop around to see which bank offers the best deal and work the costs into your business and pricing, but like my photographer friend it could make the difference between having customers or no business.

Just look at the restaurant business. How many of us would still go into a restaurant if they didn't accept our debit or credit cards?

Include a mail order facility

I believe every business that sells a product should have way customers buy their goods via mail order.

Let's go back to the homemade soap business example again.

Here you are selling a unique, desirable product to customers who visit your shop, stand, stall or car boot. Chances are that many of these customers do not live in your immediate area and probably won't be able to return to buy some more. The product itself can be posted almost anywhere relatively inexpensively, which makes it ideal for mail order. Yet an amazing number of businesses ignore the potential additional sales that mail order can bring.

◆ TIP ◆

If you are retailing your product and it is capable of being posted, then why not offer it mail order?

Nothing fancy is needed

All that's needed is to include a small advertisement somewhere, either on the outer packaging or on a small note inside, telling your customer that if they're delighted with their purchase, which you trust they will be, then they can order more either via your website or phoning you direct.

You can also use this as an opportunity to promote all the other products you do that your customer may not yet have bought. And in the unlikely event that your customer is not satisfied with their purchase you can ask them to email you with their comments.

By adding mail order to your business you really can increase sales without paying out for further advertising because previous customers will now be able to buy again from you, and will almost certainly start recommending you to their friends, colleagues, and family and this in turn builds further sales.

Customer loyalty schemes are now commonplace amongst the country's largest retailers. There's nothing to stop you introducing similar schemes in your business. And if you have a website where customers can sign up for your regular free newsletter you can include all sorts of things like details of your latest products, competitions and so on.

Offer customer referral incentives

The insurance business relies heavily on successfully targeting their existing satisfied customers to introduce them to new customers, often in areas where previously they have been unsuccessful.

Referrals work on the basis that if your customers are happy with your products and services, they should be encouraged to recommend your business to everyone they think might benefit from what you're offering.

Usually a tempting incentive is offered, which could be anything from a pen to a gift voucher or even a holiday. As soon as the nominated friend buys something, whoever referred them gets their gift as a thank you.

◆ TIP ◆

Encouraging referrals by offering incentives is a great way of building up your customer base at a fraction of what it would cost using traditional advertising methods.

Sales leads generated from this type of campaign are far easier to turn into actual sales because the people you will be selling to will be more open to buying your products as you've come via personal introduction.

It's easy to introduce referral schemes
All you have to do is ask your existing customers to recommend someone they know to receive a copy of your latest brochure, sample product, newsletter etc, and as soon as this nominated person starts shopping they will receive their free gift.

To really make this system work you need to create a sense of urgency. Otherwise your campaign runs the risk of suffering from 'I'll do it tomorrow' syndrome. The most effective way of getting your existing customers to recommend someone today is to set a deadline when the offer runs out. Of course there's nothing to stop you then re-running the offer at a later date when hopefully you will get another batch of potential clients.

Ways to make your referral scheme work
1. Offer a desirable gift, but something that is not going to cost your business a fortune. For example you could offer a gift voucher that can be redeemed against future orders. The advantage here is that not only are you getting new customers referred to your business, but you are also encouraging existing customers to buy again so they can use the gift voucher.

2. Set a deadline for when the offer expires. Remember that to make this scheme work you need to create a sense of urgency. Your aim is to get your customers referring their friends to you within a certain period of time if they are to qualify for their incentive.

3. As soon as you get your new customers shopping with you offer them a similar incentive to refer their friends and so on.

4. Keep interest alive by varying your incentives. Gift vouchers are fine for one occasion but try and offer something different next time.

5. Consider introducing a rewards points system where points are awarded for every new customer introduced who spends a minimum predetermined amount. Points are also awarded on future purchases and once a certain number of points have been accumulated a larger incentive gift can be claimed.

Whatever type of business you are planning to start, make sure you introduce some sort of referral scheme, even if it's just to ask your customers if they know of anyone else who would benefit from what you're offering.

Publish your own newsletter

Newsletters are a great way of promoting your own products, keeping your customers loyal and generating additional income for your business by either selling advertising space or earning commission on selling others' goods.

Already got your website?

If you have a website, publishing your own electronic newsletter, or e-zine, is relatively straightforward. (See Chapter 8 for more information.)

The advantages of having an online newsletter is that you'll get potential customers as well as existing customers signing up. For example, I run a *Top Tips For Gardeners* newsletter via one of my websites, and I get as many would-be customers as customers signing up. The challenge is then to convert the would-bes into customers while encouraging my existing customers to recommend my products and services to everyone they know.

If you haven't got a website

You don't need to have a website to publish your own newsletter. What you do need, however, is a customer address list to send it to. This isn't a problem in my gardening business where I automatically get potential customers' names and addresses when they phone up asking me to go and give them a quote.

Building your mailing list

But if you're selling your goods at craft fairs, exhibitions and other retail outlets the chances are you won't be able to get names and addresses. Don't despair – there's a simple way around this. All you have to do is include a copy of your current newsletter with everyone's purchase. Make sure also that you give a copy to anyone who browses your stand. The trick here is to get as many copies of your newsletter out as possible.

The easiest and most effective way of getting people to send you their details and subscribe to your newsletter is to offer an incentive. Again there are a number of things you can offer here, for example, gift voucher with 10 per cent off first purchase, free goody bag, pen, holdall etc, but I believe the most irresistible incentive is to run a competition.

Your competition

It is vital here that you have a worthwhile enough prize for people to want to enter so give it some thought and be prepared to splash out a little. Here's how it works. Give your readers a question to answer. Make sure you include a cut-out coupon for them to complete.

Make sure your cut-out coupon collects the following information.

1. full name;

2. date of birth (*important so you can get a feel of the age group who buy, or are interested in, your products and services. Also useful if you are to send them a card on their birthday*);

3. address including postcode;

4. email address;

5. telephone number.

Remember, the objective of running the competition is to get people to sign up for your newsletter, so don't forget to ask them to subscribe. Something along the lines of:

Please tick here ☐ if you would *not* like to receive our newsletter completely free of charge delivered regularly to your letterbox.

I recommend you ask them to tick the box if they don't want to receive your newsletter because market research indicates that this is the most effective way of getting people to agree to something.

You could of course simply ask them to tick the box if they would like to receive your regular newsletter free of charge. It's up to you.

If you're thinking about offering a relatively high-value prize then don't feel that the draw must take place prior to your next newsletter coming out. This needn't be the case. You can run the competition over any period you want, provided you indicate when the competition closes.

For example, you could start your competition in spring and say, 'Lucky winner to be announced in the winter edition of this newsletter,' which shouldn't have any adverse effect on entries.

Designing and publishing your newsletter
You don't have to go to enormous expense to run a successful newsletter. For my gardening business I publish a seasonal newsletter using a software program on my PC. You don't even have to go to that extent if you don't want to. Provided your document is well laid out, easy to read and attractive then that's fine.

You can get it photocopied or if you have a large mailing list, it's probably cheaper and more efficient to have it done by your local printer.

What makes a good newsletter?

There are two angles you must consider here.

1. Your needs: to make this publication sell more of your products and services and expand your customer client base.

2. Your customer's needs: they've got to get something from reading your newsletter. If they don't they won't read it, and everyone loses out.

It's vital the **content** of your newsletter is informative and interesting in a chatty sort of way. Few, if any, will want to read a newsletter which sounds like an advertisement, or talks down to them.

So you need to work on your content. Make sure your newsletter includes interesting, and if possible previously unknown, facts about your products or services.

For example, my *Top Tips For Gardeners* newsletter always includes something about the flowers and plants that are in bloom at the time. My last spring issue contained the following information about daffodils:

> Did you know that daffodil bulbs were used by the Roman surgeons to treat a gladiator's open wounds and gashes?
>
> And Roman soldiers always carried daffodil bulbs in their knapsacks when going to war?
>
> When eaten daffodil bulbs suppress the nervous system, so it's thought that the soldiers used the bulbs not only to treat their wounds, but give them courage!
>
> How are your daffodils looking this year?

I then go on to give five top tips for caring for daffodils and what to do after they've flowered.

I finish this piece by inviting my readers to contact me to arrange for our company to come around and prepare their garden ready for the spring. Because January is usually a quiet month for us, as it is for many businesses, I offer an incentive.

> Winter Warmer – Book your spring tidy up before 31 January and we'll give you 10% off our normal rates. Book today on (telephone number) to take advantage of this special offer.

Note that I've created a sense of urgency by asking customers to book before 31 January. This creates a sense of urgency and also means I don't have to discount any work which comes in February, the month our business traditionally picks up.

Some things you could include in your newsletter:

◆ **Any interesting history** behind your products: how did your products get their name? Where were they first sold? Anyone famous using these products? What's the most expensive one to ever have been sold?

◆ **Other customers' tips and advice.** Invite your readers to write and share their tips and advice with others. This works well with hobby businesses where there is a natural sense of allegiance because everyone is interested in the same thing.

◆ **Your business diary.** If you're planning to exhibit at a certain venue, let your customers know in advance by way of your newsletter. Again you could offer an incentive – bring along your copy of this month's newsletter and get your free gift etc.

◆ **Staff profiles.** If you're hiring staff you could include a different staff profile in each issue. Especially if you're offering a mail order service you could introduce your clients to the person or people responsible for taking their orders.

◆ **Product advice.** Tell your readers how to get the most out of what they've bought. Depending on your business you can include all sorts of helpful information here.

- **How to guides**. Write your own short 'how to' guides for your hobby. Even though the object of my gardening newsletter is to sell more of our products and services, I like to include short garden guides. The feedback is always positive and if nothing else it provides you with an opportunity to demonstrate your skills and knowledge.

- **Now is the time to...** Somewhere in your newsletter you should always include a '...now is the time to' feature, especially if things have some sort of natural deadline. For example if you're running walking holidays in Cornwall and you know that fairly soon your next month's diary will be full – then tell your customers: 'Anyone considering booking their walking holiday in July should do so now as there are only a few places left.' Or, 'You really only have two weeks left to plant your onion sets if you want to have them in time for summer salad days.'

◆ **TIP** ◆

My advice is to keep it short. You're not printing a magazine or newspaper, so keep it as short as possible. Aim to leave your readers wanting more rather than having them put it down halfway through.

What about pictures?

If you're publishing an online newsletter then you can include picture links in your newsletter. But be careful: depending on your connection it's not always easy to download pictures and they can distract from the main content.

If you want to include pictures in your online newsletter then the best way is either to write in some hyperlinks, which are links either to other websites or web pages, at end of the newsletter, or tell your readers there are now new pictures on your website.

For paper newsletters, I'd recommend you steer away from pictures. I think it's too expensive and doesn't really fit in with what's normally expected of a newsletter.

If you can't write your own

If you really can't write your own newsletter then try to get a friend, relative, partner or even a member of your staff involved with it. Discuss with them what you're looking for and what you hope to achieve by having a newsletter. Get yourself online and sign up to a few newsletters so you can get a feel for what they're about.

But do try to include them in your business. A well-written, regular newsletter is a great way of turbo-boosting your sales, and at a fraction of the cost of traditional advertising.

Making it 'sticky'

Good newsletters are sticky ones. By sticky I mean that not only do your customers read them every month but they find they can't do without them.

There are a number of ways you can make your newsletter sticky:

◆ **Competitions**. Run regular competitions where you announce the winner in a future issue. You print the lucky winner's name and they have to contact you within so many days to claim their prize.

◆ **Reader's notice board**. Invite your readers to advertise their items for sale in your newsletter. My advice is not to charge them for this service as you'll benefit from having a more interesting and stickier publication.

◆ **Ongoing feature**. Choose an interesting area of your hobby and write an ongoing feature as opposed to simply writing it all in one go. Divide it up into, say, four parts. Remember to finish each piece with a taster of what's to come in the next issue.

Naming your publication

Just like when choosing the name for your business, spend a bit of time working on a title for your newsletter.

Originally I called my gardening newsletter *From the Potting Shed*, but when I asked readers what they most liked about it, they said the tips.

So I simply call it *Top Tips For Gardeners*. It may sound a bit uninspiring and unoriginal, but it does what it says on the tin because every issue is packed full of useful tips, advice and information for gardeners.

Finally!

Remember the objective of publishing your newsletter is twofold:

1. By reading your newsletter your customer should get some interesting information and details of special offers, new products etc.

2. You in turn should get increased business and customer loyalty.

Send a card

Another great way to ensure customer loyalty and boost sales is to send your clients cards, which can include:

♦ Christmas cards
♦ Birthday cards
♦ Postcards
♦ Get well soon cards

Sending Christmas cards to all your customers can increase your sales by up to 20 per cent.

Christmas cards

In our businesses we send cards to all our customers and also to those who have expressed previous interest in our business. The results are often amazing and I believe that not only do we continue to keep our customers by sending them cards but we win lots of new business, too.

Birthday cards

Earlier we looked at the sort of information you should ask for when getting customers to sign up for your newsletter. This included asking for date of birth so you've no excuse for not sending your clients a birthday card. You could also consider sending them a small gift in appreciation of their business.

Postcards

It might seem an unusual thing to send your customers, but postcards make great inexpensive marketing tool for announcing special offers, end of line reductions etc. You could have your own postcards printed using a picture of your products or something else that depicts your business, or just use off-the-shelf postcards with images relevant to your business.

Other cards

Where you're running a business where you get to know your customers and meet them on a regular basis, such as a gardening business, you can send all sorts of other cards including get well soon cards and congratulations cards. When I hear that one of my gardening customers is unwell I always send them a get well soon card. These are the small, inexpensive touches that sets your business apart from the rest.

◆ TIP ◆

Cards are a powerful and relatively inexpensive sales tool. Saying thank you is one way of making sure your customers stay loyal to you and your business.

SUMMARY

1. You don't have to be an expert to be a successful salesperson.

2. The most successful sales strategy in the world is simply to ask for the order.

3. People buy benefits, not features.

4. Objections are buying signals.

5. A professional salesperson will recognise buying signals and work on them to achieve a sale.

6. Turbo-boost your business sales by taking credit and debit cards; offering mail order; client referral schemes; publishing your own newsletter; and sending customers, both existing and potential, cards.

7. Selling – there really is nothing to fear.

6

The Essentials of Shoestring Marketing

One of the most difficult things to get right when starting a new business is knowing how to market your new venture.

Unfortunately it's an area often overlooked. Efforts can vary from large and expensive magazine advertisements to doing absolutely nothing at all. Often both approaches bring the same result. Nothing happens.

WHY IS MARKETING SO IMPORTANT?

Having a successful marketing strategy for your business is like having a powerful train driving customers through your doors. Once these customers are through your doors, you can then work on selling them your goods and services. All too often businesses concentrate their efforts on the sales function without really bothering about marketing, which results in poor sales because customers aren't coming to buy.

I am going to assume that you don't have thousands of pounds to spend on marketing. Even if you have a large budget available, be forewarned that the amount you spend on marketing your business does not necessarily equal the size of your sales.

LEARNING FROM LARGER BUSINESSES

Before we look at marketing techniques, I want to tell you about an excellent, free way of getting up-to-the-minute telesales training. Every year big businesses invest millions of pounds training their telesales staff in the latest techniques for telemarketing. As soon as you open your business, you will get bombarded with all sorts of people trying to sell you something. Personally, I never buy anything over the phone; even if it's something that I'm interested in I will only decide if and when I see written information including terms and conditions.

But rather than get annoyed at this constant stream of telesales people, see them as offering you a free telesales course. After all, they will be sharing with you all the expensive training they have been given. Of course the standard of call will vary from awful to brilliant, but either way you can learn from these people.

What you'll learn from telesales executives

How to approach a cold sales telephone call
You'll learn a lot from how they work the call so as to get through to the decision maker. Obviously the last thing they want to do is waste their time selling advertising space to someone who is not a decision maker.

So listen to how they make their initial approach. What distinguishes professional telesales executives from the others you'll get calling you is that the pro will have their homework done. They'll have the name of who they want to speak to. The amateurs or no-hopers will simply say something like, 'Hello, can I speak to the business owner, please?' or another favourite, 'Can I speak to the person who handles the utility bills...?'

How to overcome common objections
The reason I urge you to tell them you're not interested is because then you'll learn how to handle initial objections. The most important thing when handling any objection is to keep dialogue going and build up a relationship because people find it more difficult to say no to someone they like.

The more objections you raise the better the lesson becomes. I've used many of their techniques with great effect in my own business.

Coping with rejection

Whatever business you're planning to start you're going to have to learn to handle rejection as you're going to get it. Often in truck loads. When a professional telesales executive calls you and you make it clear you don't want whatever it is they're selling you, they won't take it personally. 'Well thank you very much for your time this morning, Mr Power, I appreciate how busy you are, but if you ever do change your mind...'

Professionals will be unfailingly polite, respectful of your time and also will try to leave the door open by saying something like, 'Would you mind if I give you a call, let's say in a couple of months, to see if your situation has changed?'

If they sound nice and reasonable the chances are you'll probably say yes. From their point of view they've succeed in one goal at least – keeping the door open.

WHY ADVERTISING DOESN'T WORK

Small businesses waste thousands of pounds annually on expensive advertising that will never bring them a single customer. Unfortunately many labour under the misconception that all they have to do to bring business through their doors is go with the biggest ad they can afford. Advertising doesn't work this way.

For an advertisement to work it must have a clear, quantifiable objective, nothing as vague as 'to bring in more business' or 'to increase sales'.

The advertisement's objective must be:

- **Specific.** How many new customers do you want to generate? How many products do you want to sell?

◆ **Measurable**. How are you going to work out how successful your ad is? One way is to ask to customers replying to your ad to quote a specific reference number or mention the ad itself to take advantage of a special offer.

◆ **Targeted**. You must make sure your ad is going to reach your potential market. If you're a hairdresser offering a mobile hairdressing service, you need to target those people who for whatever reasons find themselves mostly housebound.

The key to success is to make sure the objective is achievable.

Too many advertisements are dead simply because they can't achieve what's expected of them. For example, a common, and easily made, mistake is to use a small advertisement to try to sell your products. A single advertisement can't do this.

So the objective for the advertisements we run for our Dutch bikes is to get people motivated to get further information on our products. They can do this by either visiting our website or phoning us for a brochure.

Rather than see your advertisement as simply a tool for selling your goods, instead use it as a vehicle for bringing potential customers to either your telephone line or website to find out more about your products and services. This way at least your advertisement stands some chance of achieving its objective.

A word about advertising sales executives

Beware, be very aware, that when someone phones you to sell you advertising space their primary concern is to make a sale for their business not necessarily to generate increased business for your company.

Imagine for a moment someone rings you completely out of the blue to tell you all about something great that they say will do your business the power of good. It's expensive, but you agree to go ahead convinced that the investment is worth is because your sales will rocket. You pay your money (unless you've a trading history, most ads have to be paid for upfront) and you wait in eager anticipation until the day of publication.

Absolutely nothing happens – you fail to get even a single inquiry via your expensive advertisement. This scenario isn't as uncommon as you think. It's one that's happened to me in my business and from speaking to other entrepreneurs it's happened to them, too.

◆ EXPERIENCE ◆

Recently we approached a large glossy gardening magazine to run a specific series of advertisements promoting one of our business's new products. I spent considerable time on the phone with the sales executive discussing our advertisement's objective. The salesperson agreed that not only would our ad do well in their publication but that they would also be willing to do a feature on our product.

Our first ad came and went with a dismal response. Having already sent a sample of our product to the magazine's editor, I was surprised that I had heard nothing. So I phoned and was told they never received it (although they had received the covering letter, which was odd). Undeterred, I sent another sample of our product hoping for the promised review.

The next issue of the magazine arrived and our product had still not been reviewed. Much to my annoyance our competitors' product had, and they hadn't even advertised in the magazine.

When I phoned the magazine for an explanation I was told that the editor did not think that our product was suitable for their readership. But their advertising department had assured me our product was ideal for their readership.

I pulled our advertisement immediately despite warnings from the sales manager that we would be liable to pay for further ads as we had entered into a contract.

Naturally I pointed out that under such circumstances they'd have a struggle to convince a court that we owed them money.

I cannot stress enough that the only thing an advertising executive is interested in is their commission and their publication's future. Your business is simply a means to an end. Don't rely on anything they tell you and make sure that your products and services are right for their magazine. While the offer of a cheap advertisement might seem attractive, it becomes very expensive when you don't get any business from it.

My favourite method for promoting our businesses is using our websites. This is covered fully in Chapter 8.

Here are my preferred shoestring offline marketing techniques.

TEN WAYS TO MARKET YOUR BUSINESS WITH A SMALL BUDGET

1. Classified advertisements.
2. Press releases.
3. Sponsorship.
4. Media stunts.
5. Make more use of your business cards.
6. Join a local networking group.
7. Use self-employed sales agents.
8. Leaflet drops.
9. Give talks to other businesses.
10. Write for your favourite hobby magazines or create your own newsletter.

Classified advertisements

You may wonder why after berating advertisements I'm now including them in my list. My reasons are simply that some businesses will have to employ traditional advertising methods to get started and bring potential customers through their doors.

Small, and relatively inexpensive classified ads, can be an excellent, cheap way of achieving sales targets.

However, before rushing off to place your advertisements there are two very important things you must get right.

1. The publication must be suitable for your advertisement.

2. The advertisement must be as powerful as a train in pulling customers through your doors.

Is the publication's readership suitable for your advertisement?
Remember the editor who rejected our product as being unsuitable for her readership. She was right. It was unsuitable, which was why our advertisement achieved nothing. Obviously had I given it more thought and really identified who the magazine's targeted readership was, I would have come to the same conclusions as she did and not wasted our money.

If your ad is going to achieve anything for your business it must reach your target market.

When considering a publication always get a copy of the magazine or newspaper before placing your advertisement. Remember, if your advertisement is to have even the slightest hope of succeeding, your products or services must appeal to the bulk of the magazine's readers. If it doesn't your message will fail to reach your target audience.

♦ You don't have to buy the magazine or newspaper. Phone the classified sales department and ask them to send you a back issue and a media pack.

♦ The media pack will contain information on how many copies are distributed and an analysis of the typical readership.

♦ When you receive your copy go through all the advertisements and ask yourself if what you're offering is the same as what is being advertised.

- ◆ If the answer is no, or you've got your doubts, then it isn't for you. Ignore what the sales staff say. Their job is to sell advertising space, not your products.

How much should you spend?

Rates are based upon a number of factors, which include how many copies are sold monthly, quarterly or yearly, whether the magazine is a glossy colour affair or in more of a newspaper format etc. My advice is that you should initially ignore how much your advertisement is going to cost you until you've first assessed the publication's suitability.

My own experience has been that it's far too tempting to place adverts in publications which offer the best rates, while ignoring the key factor, which is do your customers read this publication? If you're sure that they do – having first worked through the existing advertisements, then you need to work out an advertising budget. The reason this is important is that you need to make sure that you don't overspend unnecessarily.

Don't be surprised when you phone the advertising department of the publication to be told that the attractive introductory offer in the publication isn't the price you'll end up paying. For instance, most will charge you extra for a colour ad and will inevitably try to sell you a larger ad than the one you had planned.

Advertorial

Whenever you do decide to go with a particular publication make sure to ask them to run a small feature about you and your business. Many will, but only if you ask them. An advertorial is a great way of getting additional publicity for your business because it's your ad dressed up as a news story.

Working out a budget

Generally speaking, any advertisement will take some time before it starts to work. Some marketing experts reckon that it can take customers as much as five exposures to your message before they will consider buying what you're offering.

If you doubt this, next time you watch television make a note of how often the same advertisement will come on during your favourite programme or a night's viewing. Anywhere between three and five seems to be the magic number. So if you're planning to run just one ad in one publication then you may as well as forget it and save your money.

I have found that it usually takes about three months of advertising in a monthly magazine before I see any return on my investment. Of course it may take longer, but I make a point of reviewing our advertisements every three months and those that aren't performing well are either axed completely or revised.

When working out your budget try to come up with a six-month or annual marketing budget. Then make sure you to stick to it. It's so easy to get carried away with bigger and better ads in the vain hope that this strategy will reap rewards. It won't and it doesn't.

◆ TIP ◆

Work out a budget that you can comfortably afford – and stick to it.

Writing a killer classified advertisement

Only after you have carefully assessed the publication's suitability for your business should you think about writing a classified ad that will hook your customers.

Five steps to writing a powerful classified advertisement:

1. Don't try to sell them anything.
2. Create a killer headline.
3. Offer something irresistible.
4. Call them to action.
5. Create a sense of urgency.

Don't try to sell them anything

Strange, but true. Rather than see your classified ad as a way to sell your products and services to potential customers, try instead to view it as a powerful train bringing carriage loads of soon-to-be customers to your business.

The primary objective of your advertisement should be to bring in enquiries and not sales. Succeed with this objective and then you can successfully sell to them when they visit your shop, website or request a copy of your mail order catalogue.

Create a killer headline

Without it your advertisement is going nowhere.

Some years ago when the Internet was still a mystery to most, I was commissioned by our local paper to write a piece on Christmas shopping on the Internet.

My feature was duly published and those I spoke to afterwards said they hadn't seen it. Even when I told them what page it had appeared on they still had difficulty finding it.

The reason? The headline. It was written assuming that readers had already some knowledge of the World Wide Web with the heading: 'Christmas Shopping on the Web', which meant nothing to most people and so they either consciously, or subconsciously, didn't read it.

◆ **TIP** ◆

Your headline must grab the reader and make them want to read more.

Target your customers by making the heading as specific as you possibly can. If your product will only appeal to those interested in sailing then make it shout at sailors:

ATTENTION FRUSTRATED SAILORS

Or if you're selling to gardeners with bad backs:

IS YOUR GARDEN BREAKING YOUR BACK?

And so on. Be as specific as you can. Grab their attention and make them want to read your ad.

Offer something irresistible

In the chapter on selling I've told you the key to all selling is that people buy benefits and not features. This is also true when it comes to your advertising.

The only way that people will be motivated to bother looking at your website, visit your shop or phone for a brochure, is if your advertisement answers their overriding motivation, which is: What's in it for me?

Following your attention-grabbing headline you must give them a powerful, irresistible benefit.

The way to do this is to write down all the benefits that someone would get if they bought what you're offering. We're not just looking for unique selling points here, we're looking for benefits, which could include:

◆ cheapest in the market;
◆ sole supplier of such a product;
◆ only a few products left – after that you won't be able to repeat these prices;
◆ only so many vacancies left – after that you are full for the rest of the year.

The next step is to prioritise your benefits and decide which one of all them is the most appealing. Highlight this one and then check through the other ads in the publication you are considering and make sure you're not duplicating someone else's advertisement.

When you've got your powerful benefit it can follow your headline:

> ### IS YOUR GARDEN BREAKING YOUR BACK?
> Our catalogue is full of products specially designed
> to take the hard work out of gardening.

Now you've got your powerful heading and created an irresistible benefit, most gardeners will be tempted to request a copy of your catalogue.

But they'll put the magazine down intending to phone you later and then something else will grab their attention, and fairly soon your ad will be part of pile of papers bound for the recycling centre.

Call them to action

To avoid this happening you must call them to action.

Next time you watch television, listen to commercial radio or pick up a magazine, listen out for the advertiser calling you to action. Car insurance companies are probably the least subtle of all. Many command you to pick up your phone right now and find out how much money they can save you on your insurance renewal. These advertisements shout at you to do something. The reason you do, is because they have already told you the all-important what's in it for you – cheaper car insurance, a cheap holiday in the sun etc.

Don't be afraid to be bold and blunt (without of course being offensive). Something like:

> *Our catalogue is full of products specially designed to take the hard work out of gardening. Copies are limited so order now to avoid disappointment.*

Create a sense of urgency

The response to your call to action can be greatly improved if you create a sense of urgency as well. There are a number of ways you can do this, for example:

◆ offer a free gift with every catalogue requested before a certain date;
◆ offer a discount on all lines for orders placed before a certain date;
◆ make 'only while stocks last' announcements;
◆ offer give-away prices for a specific period only.

Remember that the primary objective of your advertisement is to bring customers through your doors so create as much urgency as you can by offering a powerful time-sensitive incentive. You don't have to offer discounts on all your products or services. One will do so long as it's powerful enough to pull them through the doors.

The worst-case scenario for your ad is to have either no one see it to begin with – more common that you think – or for potential customers to read it and not be motivated to find out more.

Spend as much time as you can working on your classified advertisement. Look at it from the perspective of your potential customers and not your own. Keep the 'What's in it for me?' motivating factor at the forefront of everything you do.

Get it right and a small, relatively inexpensive, classified advertisement can see your sales rocket and guarantee your business's future success.

Don't worry if you don't get it right first time. Review and revise your advertisement as necessary and remember it can take months before you see any great return on your ad.

PRESS RELEASES

A press release is a marketing tool that is often overlooked by small business owners and is still my favourite.

Nothing will generate sales quicker than a favourable mention in your hobby magazine, local newspaper, radio or television channel, and it's not as difficult as you might imagine. Although obviously the greater your understanding and knowledge of how to write your press releases the greater your chances of success.

Read as much as you can about this subject, but don't be intimidated by the word 'press' or be afraid to contact the media with your ideas.

A simple, effective press release

Every day newspaper editors, magazine editors and television producers are deluged with press releases from businesses, politicians, entertainers and more, all trying to get publicity for their interests.

The reason they want to be featured on the news is that people are more receptive to their sales message via the news as opposed to advertisements.

However, editors aren't in the business of running free ads for anyone and they know that if their publication, television or radio programme has even the slightest hint of promoting products and services people will turn off in their droves. So the golden rule when it comes to approaching any media publication is to remember that editors buy news and their publications sell advertisement space.

So to succeed in getting your business featured in their publications, your press release must contain something that is newsworthy and not simply seen as promoting your business. Once you know where to look you'll soon find lots of potential angles for a news story.

Although most local newspapers are pleased to run a small piece on a new business opening in the area, you won't find the glossy monthly magazines quite as accommodating.

Even so, prior to launching your business you should always contact the editor of your local newspaper and also the editor of any magazine that covers your hobby or interest. But when contacting them you must be able to offer them a powerful benefit for featuring your business. After all, what you're doing here is selling them a news item or something interesting and unique that will appeal to their readers or viewers.

What's newsworthy about your business?

1. **Human interest.** All news revolves around human interest. Although you might think that an innovative new product is a newsworthy item, it's worthless unless it has a human-interest angle.

   Imagine for a moment that you've just found a new product that overcomes sea sickness. Simply writing a press release announcing this fact isn't going to grab anyone's attention or imagination unless you can work it into a human interest story. So rather than saying 'Hey, we've just found the perfect solution to curing seasickness,' you would announce that either you or someone you know who has suffered from seasickness has finally found relief from this awful condition.

   The product is the solution, but the story an editor would be interested in is the impact it's had on a previous sufferer.

2. **Previous career or occupation.** Your previous career may well be a news story on its own. For example, a former city banker trading his suit and tie for the kitchen and happily running his own organic catering business is a great story for the contrast in careers. People love to read about how others have changed their lives, especially those who've swapped a high-flying career for something completely different.

3. **Employment and local prosperity.** There isn't an editor in the country who would turn down a story where a new business was going to further enhance an area's reputation, or create new jobs. Stories like these are sought after. So if you're going to be improving an area and offering more employment and greater prosperity – there's your angle.

4. **Gaps in the market.** With every hobby there is something that is either difficult to get, or prohibitively expensive to do. For example,

as anyone who owns a boat knows, mooring fees have reached an all-time high. Incredible as it may sound many boat owners are now moving their boats abroad, away from UK marinas, as berthing rates are far more affordable.

A marina near where I lived introduced an innovative solution by offering low cost 'dry berth moorings', something which is popular in the US. Rather than have a berth for your boat, it is dry stored at the marina when you're not using it. As soon as you want to go boating you phone and the marina arranges to have your boat ready in the water for you. Once you've finished it is then lifted and dry stored again. The advantage to everyone is that the cost of dry berth is extremely favourable compared with a traditional water berth.

Because the marina was offering an innovative way of reducing the cost of berthing, the story was taken up in all the press including the local television news.

There are literally thousands of ways your business could be newsworthy; all you have to do is work out the best ones. Remember the key to success is looking for the human-interest angle.

◆ TIP ◆

No one will be interested in a product or service alone. It's the 'What's in it for me?' angle you're looking for.

Issuing a press release

Once you've found your news item you'll need to communicate it to the editors of the various media you intend to contact.

Many books will recommend you use a set format for your press release, I recommend you don't. Instead, try something that doesn't smack of attempting to get free publicity – rather offer the editor an irresistible story to win favour with their readers.

A simple but effective press release is to write a letter to the editor. The big advantage of doing this is that if the editor doesn't include a piece on your business, hopefully your letter will still appear in the readers' letters section. This is not to be scoffed at, as this is usually the most read section in any publication.

My experience has been that I make my letter as compelling as I possibly can. I include a 'call to action' for the editor at the end of the letter asking them to contact me for more information or to come and visit us for a coffee and a tour of what we're about.

The results are usually positive and I've found that either the editor or a staff journalist has phoned me to find out more information, and then done a nice interesting feature on our business.

What to include
1. That all-important headline.
2. What's special about your business.
3. Briefly how it started.
4. A bit about you.
5. Call to action.

The headline
Just like a classified ad, you will need to make it attention grabbing, but without looking tacky and cheap.

What's special about your business
This is where you describe why you are newsworthy – what makes what you're doing unique and of interest to the publication's readers.

Briefly how it started
It's important to cover this, as often this is where the editor's interest lies. A former estate agent swapping selling houses for opening a herb farm is more interesting than the herbs themselves. The life-changing angle will appeal to more people than the fact that the area is to get a new herb farm.

A bit about you

What's your vision for the future? Would you like to see everyone eating delicious healthy herbs and getting wonderful benefits? Be bold here. This might be the paragraph that gives the editor the news story he wants.

Call to action

End your letter with a powerful call to action. Something like 'Pick up your phone now and I'll tell you all about it,' probably won't work. So try something like inviting the paper to come and visit your new business to try out your new product or service – it is an ideal way of calling an editor to action.

Contacting other media

Television and radio stations are always on the lookout for local and national news stories.

Our local ITV news runs regular features on small local businesses, which have included boat builders, dolls house makers, book enthusiasts, people who run walking holidays and even a man who makes pub models from things he finds in the local tip.

◆ TIP ◆

Don't be afraid to contact your local TV or radio station. You'll often find they ask anyone with a story to contact them.

Approach TV and radio in same way you would a newspaper or magazine. Again, try to avoid a formal press release style format and go for a more personal approach. You're far more likely to get a positive response if you come across as friendly and enthusiastic as opposed to trying to act like a large corporation.

SPONSORSHIP

There are all sorts of good causes out there that would be delighted to receive sponsorship from a local business. You could sponsor anything from a local football team to building and maintaining a flower border or garden for a hospice or children's home.

Not only are you doing something worthwhile, but also getting some excellent publicity for your business.

You needn't just sponsor charities. There is a now a growing trend amongst budget-conscious local authorities to invite businesses to sponsor the upkeep and maintenance of everything from roundabouts to local parks and gardens.

Having a nice big sign on one of the roundabouts leading into your town or city is a great way of promoting your business.

Whatever your hobby, there will be some group glad of the financial and inspirational help of a business involved in the same field.

◆ TIP ◆

Sponsorship is a win-win situation.

Every year our business sponsors a worthwhile cause. Not only are we making a difference and getting a great feel-good factor for doing so, we are also raising the profile of our business locally.

MEDIA STUNTS

Richard Branson is arguably the current king of the media stunt machine and we can all learn from his successful strategies.

Contrary to the image of journalists portrayed in films where they're constantly running around searching out that all-important story, most journalists haven't the time or resources necessary to do this. Instead, they look for ready-made stories via their contacts at hospitals, police stations, council offices, undertakers and the like. When they find something they believe would be of interest to their publication's readers they then work on the story.

Although this method is usually successful, the problem arises in that their rival publication makes the same phone calls every day. Editors are aware of this and are obviously keen to either have a different slant on local news stories, or to look for something completely different.

> Doing something unique and inviting the local media to come and witness your stunt is a great way of generating instant publicity.

Let's imagine for a moment that you're planning to run walking holidays but are finding that many of the rights of ways in your area have been blocked by local landowners. Obviously their actions will have a negative impact on your business as your walkers will be unable to follow what are often the more interesting routes.

You could arrange for a local protest where you and a bunch of walking enthusiasts set out to challenge the actions of the local landowners.

Doing this will accomplish two objectives. The first thing you might achieve is to open up public walks which should already be accessible to the public. Provided you contact as many of the local press as you can you will also be assured of getting great publicity.

There are all sorts of stunts you can arrange for your business to generate publicity. Think big!

MAKING MORE USE OF YOUR BUSINESS CARDS

I have a simple philosophy when it comes to business cards – you can never give out enough of them. You'd be amazed at how quickly you can increase your sales if you start using your business cards as a marketing tool as opposed to simply a piece of information.

Before we look at the all the ways you can distribute your card, you first need to look at your existing card, or if you haven't got one, start planning what you'll need to include in it.

Designing your business card

The three deadly sins of the business card design are having:

- blank spaces;
- no sales message;
- no call to action.

Blank spaces

If you already have a business card I'd like you to take it out now and turn it over so that you can't see the print. OK? So what can you see? A blank piece of paper? Or a powerful sales message?

I'm not a betting man, but I'd lay odds that the majority of people will be staring at a blank piece of paper. Leaving one side of the business card blank is the first deadly sin of business card design.

If you were running commercial vehicles as part of your business you wouldn't leave one side of the vehicle without a sign, so why leave half your business card blank?

Most people will have had their cards printed like this because this is the way the printer does them. However for a bit more money you can have the back of your card printed with an all-important powerful call to action.

No sales message

Just like your classified advertisement, your business card should have a powerful sales message. Otherwise why would anyone want to call you?

The fact that you sell fishing gear won't be enough to get people to call you. Remember that they need to be told what's in it for them.

So rather than just telling them where your fishing tackle shop is based, tell them why they should visit your business as opposed to your competitors'. And what better place to do this than that great big blank space of the back of your business card?

Even something as simple as what I've written below is better than a blank space.

> Don't forget to visit us online and see for yourself our
> amazing range of products at prices you won't get from anywhere else.

Call to action

Now you've told them why they should visit your business you must call them to act, otherwise your card will go into the bottom of their wallet, bin or coat pocket never to be seen again.

Call us today to take advantage of our special offers.

Phone us now for a friendly chat to see how we can help you.

Quote reference BiZcard1 and claim 10% off your first order.

The sooner you get your business cards selling for you, as opposed to simply providing information, the better. If you already have 250 business cards with a blank space, no sales message and no call to action then you should consider having some reprinted.

Distributing your card

You should never miss an opportunity to hand out your card. For example:

- Enclose your business card with every bill you pay or correspondence you reply to.

- Get your business card on every notice board, window or wall where people gather and wait. For example, barber shops, dentists' surgeries, restaurants, bars, staff rooms, shop notice boards – anywhere you're allowed to put your card up.

◆ Whenever you meet a prospective customer don't simply give them your card, personalise it. If they ask the price of something, write it down on your card as opposed to simply telling them, or worse still writing in on a scrap piece of paper.

◆ Even if everyone knows about your business, it's still worth giving friends and relatives a quantity of your business cards so they can give them to their colleagues and friends and put them up in their local barbers and so on.

LOCAL NETWORKING GROUPS

This may not suit every business, but networking groups are a useful way of building up local business contacts.

Groups generally work on the basis that you attend regular meetings, which can vary from breakfast get togethers to evening meetings where you meet other business owners and entrepreneurs just like you.

Even if you don't think that joining one of these groups will introduce you to new customers, they can still be a useful way of making excellent local contacts. For example if you're looking for funding your new business venture you could well find someone at these events.

If nothing else, it's a good way of getting away from your kitchen table and getting a fresh perspective on your business.

Online networking groups

You can also network online by joining any of the online forums relating to your hobby or entrepreneurial matters. Just browsing through previous discussion threads can be an excellent way of getting new ideas and solutions to your problems.

Remember if you're having problems with a certain aspect of your business, the chances are others have experienced the same difficulties. The answer to your problems may already have been solved by someone else which will save you time, money and stress.

TIP ◆

> Online networking is an excellent way of both promoting your business and getting that all-important support.

SELF-EMPLOYED SALES AGENTS

It is worth considering whether or not your product or services can be sold either in the UK or worldwide. You can employ a network of self-employed sales agents.

Rather than rely on your own marketing efforts you can benefit from the experiences and contacts of already-established sales agents.

Lots of products and service are marketed in this way, from boats to holidays to books.

How it works

You recruit a number of motivated sales agents who will sell your products or services for which they earn a commission.

◆ **EXPERIENCE** ◆

> Let's imagine for a moment that your business is making dolls houses and that each house retails at £100. The cost of selling your product on your own can be greatly reduced if you contact existing businesses that already attract your target customers and get them to sell your dolls houses.
>
> The advantage to the sales agents is that they don't have to buy your stock. Instead you provide them with free point-of-sale material, which includes an example of your product. When their customers enquire about these houses, the sales agent will be able to answer all their questions because you will have briefed/trained them in advance. The sales agent then takes the order and the money, contacts you with the customer's details and pays you the amount they have received from their customer less the agreed commission.

Make sure that your commission structure is generous enough to be appealing while still leaving you with a worthwhile profit margin.

Where to find them

You could either approach retailers direct by telephoning, emailing or writing to them with your proposal, or you could run a classified advertisement in the business opportunity section of newspapers and magazines. Another way is to advertise that you are looking for sales agents on your website and point-of-sale material.

Does it really work?

Yes it does. In our businesses we hold a number of agents for a variety of products and we also recruit our own sales agents to sell our courses.

The reason I like using self-employed sales agents is because they are motivated by commission. If they don't sell your products, you don't pay them anything. After a short time it soon becomes apparent which agents you want to keep and invest further in and those you have to let go.

Provided you listen to what your agents are telling you, you can also get some very useful and regular feedback from customers about how your products and services can be improved.

LEAFLET DROPS

If your target customer is locally based, door-to-door leafleting is a very cost-effective way of promoting your products and services.

There are a number of options:

- do it yourself;
- employ someone to do it on your behalf;
- have your leaflet included in an existing paper, for example your local property paper or weekly advertiser.

We've used door-to-door leaflet drops with great effect in our gardening business. Personally I prefer to arrange and do it all ourselves rather than employ a company to do it. All you have to do is recruit some casual help and blitz an area.

Designing your leaflet

Your leaflet is crucial to your success. Just like all your other marketing material it must include:

- **The big offer.** Why should anyone want to use your product or service?

- **A powerful benefit to potential customers** for choosing you over your competitors.

- **Credibility.** It is vital that you establish your credibility. So if you have any qualifications or have won any awards in your particular field don't forget to mention them. If you haven't any qualifications then don't worry. You can still establish credibility by including: 'references available', 'fully insured' (if appropriate).

- **Create a sense of urgency.** For example offer a discount for anyone booking you prior to the end of the month or a special offer for new customers. Whatever you offer, make sure it has a time limit.

- **Call to action.** Never forget this crucial bit. You must tell them to do something, whether it's to call you or visit your website.

- **Your full contact details.** Unfortunately we're living in a society that seems to be dominated by rogue businesses and so we're all subject to suspicion and scrutiny. Even if you only include your name and a land-based telephone number you are greatly increasing the odds that people will call you as you're providing them with information that the rogues will never give. If you can go one step further and include your website address and office address you really are taking positive action to establish yourself as a professional. If the only contact detail you can provide is a mobile telephone number, then this type of marketing isn't for you. People are right to be suspicious of anyone providing only a mobile telephone number.

Try to make your leaflet as eye-catching and interesting as possible and always get it printed by a professional. A cheap, home-made appearance is not going to encourage anyone to call you. Shop around for a good printer and ask them if they offer a design facility. If they do, as many will, ask to see examples of their work. As soon as you see anything that resembles those awful clip-art animations then look elsewhere. You want a design that reflects your unique business and not something that looks about as inspirational as a bus ticket.

Distributing your leaflets

The benefit of leafleting is that you can target specific areas and even specific houses.

◆ **EXPERIENCE** ◆

A few years ago, I owned an Italian car, which developed an intermittent fault. Our local garage was unable to rectify it as were the other two garages I took it to. Then one weekend while the car was parked outside my house a young man put a card on the windscreen, which read: 'We specialise in repairing common faults experienced with (the manufacturer's name of my car). We also undertake servicing.'

I called the number and asked whether or not they had heard of the type of problem my car was suffering from. They told me not only had they heard of the problem but repaired these faults on a regular basis. I took the car around to them and they fixed the problem.

This is an excellent example of targeted leaflet/card marketing, which got their phones ringing every time. If you are planning to start this type of marketing, and I recommend you do if your products or services are suitable, then try to be as specific as possible both in terms of the wording on your leaflet and the area you choose to market in.

Remember the golden marketing rule – people buy benefits and not features. Make sure your leaflet or card includes a powerful and specific benefit.

What results will you get?

We regularly undertake direct leafleting in our businesses and typically we get around a 1 per cent reply rate. On occasions this can be higher, but I'd say 1 per cent is a good average. We always aim to distribute 5,000 leaflets in one marketing hit and this generates approximately 50 sales calls, which we usually receive within around three weeks of our campaign.

The times we haven't achieved these results have been those when we employed another business to do our leafleting for us. So as I said earlier, we now organise, motivate and manage our own direct marketing team.

GIVING TALKS TO GROUPS AND OTHER BUSINESSES

Whether your hobby is popular or unusual there will be always be local groups who'd love to hear you tell them more about what you're doing.

I've given talks to all sorts of local groups about gardening and garden design and have always found them an excellent way of generating new customers. When you give a talk on anything you become an expert and your credibility is immediately established. Even if those who attend your talk aren't personally in the market for your services they will tell their friends and relatives who may be, so it's worth giving everyone who attends your business card and a brochure or leaflet telling them more about what you do.

◆ TIP ◆

Many hobby enthusiasts will travel surprising distances to listen to a seasoned expert share their knowledge, experience and anecdotes.

If you're nervous about having to speak in public, don't be. There are lots of books, audio cassettes, videos and even part-time courses that you can take to turn you from nervous amateur to skilled professional. Whatever you do, don't lose out on the potential of this sort of marketing can do for your business simply because you are nervous. Any worries I've had about speaking engagements have always turned out to be groundless. My experience has been that people are wonderfully supportive, hospitable and grateful for the time I've given to them and their organisations.

Where do I find groups?

You can usually find regular updates on groups operating in your area in your local paper. Your library will also have a very useful folder containing the details of all local groups that meet in the area. Spend a bit of time going through this binder making notes of the contact names and details of any of the groups you think might be interested in a talk from you. Either write, email or phone the contact and discuss your idea with them.

Getting paid

I've never asked for a fee for speaking to groups. I believe it's a win-win situation. The group's members get to hear what I hope is an interesting and informative talk on a subject they're interested in and I get to meet potential customers for my business. I also find that I also learn new things from them. So my advice is that unless you're selling someone a course on something, you should never ask for speaking fees. But it's up to you.

WRITING FOR MAGAZINES AND NEWSPAPERS

This is similar to the idea of press releases. If in your business you're doing something different or unusual, then you should consider offering to write features for your favourite hobby magazines.

Look through any monthly gardening magazine and you will always find a business owner writing about some aspect of gardening. Whether it's a landscape gardener giving an account of how to lay the perfect lawn or a nursery owner discussing how they rid plants of common pests – it's all there.

◆ TIP ◆

Writing a feature not only gives you valuable, free publicity, but also instant credibility.

Although most magazines and newspapers pay their freelance writers and contributors, I think that if you're writing about your own business then you should not charge. After all, the costs of your taking out a 1,000 or 2,000 word advertisement would be astronomical, and beyond most of our budgets. So don't look at it that you're giving away your services free. You're not. The resulting publicity will be more than just reward.

If under any circumstances you could not consider writing a feature for a magazine, then you should still contact the magazine's editor and tell them about your business, inviting them to come along to see the insider story on how your products are made.

I love boats and nothing grabs my interest more quickly than when my favourite boating magazine visits a boat builder's and we get to see first hand how a beautiful craft is created from an idea on a piece of paper to a finished boat.

SUMMARY

Effective marketing needn't be expensive. A good website supported by a relatively inexpensive, but carefully constructed, classified ad can be far more effective than a large and expensive glossy ad. The most important thing to get right with your marketing is to begin with a budget.

Work out a figure that covers you for a series of small classified advertisements, website promotion, leaflets, business cards and any other point-of-sale material your business will require and then stick rigidly to your budget.

The most important thing to remember about advertising is that the amount of money you spend on your marketing will not guarantee you a pro-rata amount of business.

◆ **TIP** ◆

Lots of successful businesses are marketing on a shoestring. I know because ours is one of them.

So don't be afraid to go out and look for free publicity, hand out leaflets, put posters up, give talks to groups, and build your own website. Above all, take responsibility for the future of your own business and not do as many do – allow it to fall or succeed on the amount of advertising they have paid for.

1. Spending money on an advertisement will not automatically generate more business.

2. For an advertisement to work it must have a clear objective, which isn't necessarily to sell your goods.

3. A marketing campaign is one half of your sales function and is equally as important as your sales function.

4. Classified advertisements can be a great way of marketing your business.

5. Advertisements take time to work. A single ad is unlikely to give any worthwhile return.

6. Work out a marketing budget and stick to it.

7. Never buy advertisements from cold-calling telesales executives.

8. Make sure your advertisement is somewhere your target customer is visiting.

7

Deciding Where to Sell From

Regardless of how innovative or unique your products and services are you must have some sort of a shop window from which to sell. I use the words shop window loosely here as your 'shop' could be anything from a website to an ad in the small classifieds of your favourite hobby magazine.

Choosing the right venue to sell your goods is crucial to your success. Wherever you decide to sell your goods it has to satisfy the following criteria:

♦ be exposed to your target market;
♦ be affordable;
♦ allow a degree of flexibility;
♦ be secure and safe.

BE EXPOSED TO YOUR TARGET MARKET

The reason many businesses fail is not because there isn't a demand for what they're selling, but because their products and services are not marketed at those who want and need them.

◆ EXPERIENCE ◆

A few years ago a new business selling restored collectable and antique furniture opened in our town. The business owners put an enormous amount of time and effort into creating a very inviting shop which generated immediate interest. However, the shop was located in an area of the town where the neighbouring shops were late-night take-aways surrounded by housing estates.

Despite the initial interest, visitors to the shop were slow as few of the local residents were interested in what the shop was selling. Those who would have been interested didn't tend to go into the part of town where the shop was located.

Unfortunately late-night drunks became a problem and frequently the shop windows were broken by fighting and yobbish behaviour. The only way the shop owners could protect their business from these attacks was to install steel security grids over the window, which in turn meant that any hope of attracting passing window-shoppers was killed.

Sadly the business failed. The mistake here was that they set up a business in an area where they were not exposed to their target market. Why did they choose this area? Most likely because the rents here were far less than in the more affluent areas of our town, and not only were the rents lower but the retail area was far larger.

BE AFFORDABLE

Wherever you rent it must be affordable. We'll look in a moment at what's involved in taking on a shop lease, but wherever you decide to locate your business you must be sure that the products and services you're going to offer have a fair chance of generating not only enough to cover rent, rates, insurance etc, but also pay you and give a profitable return.

ALLOW A DEGREE OF FLEXIBILITY

One of the keys to running a successful business is to be flexible. You'll need to be able to adapt to market changes either as they happen, or preferably to anticipate them. If your business is located somewhere where you have no scope to change in any way – for example rearrange the sales areas, introduce or remove a workshop area – you will not be able to adapt to change and this will impact on your success.

BE SECURE AND SAFE

In the case of the antiques shop, not only was the business located in the wrong area but it was also exposed to frequent attacks. The advantages of having a shop window for your business is that passers-by can look at what you're offering and be tempted to return to your business when you are open. If you have shutters and security doors where no one can see your window displays, you are losing out on potentially valuable sales.

Some years ago a new bicycle shop opened in our area. Being a keen cyclist I was eager to have a look at what they were offering, but by the time I got home from work every day they were closed. However, they had laid out the shop in such a way you see all the lovely bicycles and their prices.

I bought a new bike from this shop a fortnight after they opened for business. This is the power of window shopping sales. I'm delighted to say that this shop is still thriving and its owners are going from strength to strength.

CHOOSING WHERE TO SELL YOUR GOODS

There are lots of places you can market your goods. Your business could include a combination of these or just one:

- website;
- space in another shop;
- concession in a retail area;
- direct marketing;
- exhibition or trade fair;
- hotel foyer;

- train station platform;
- shops, cafés and kiosk;
- boot sales or market stall;
- shop;
- local authority concession;
- an existing business.

Website

In Chapter 8 we'll cover what's involved in setting up an online business. Whatever type of business you are planning to start a website can be a great and inexpensive way of either selling your products or promoting your business.

Space in another shop

Probably the most inexpensive way of getting your own shop is to hire a space in someone else's. While this can be an ideal solution for some businesses it won't suit everyone.

The type of products most suited to this type of arrangement are:

- antiques
- collectables
- jewellery
- paintings
- restored or unusual furniture
- toys
- memorabilia
- non-perishable food items
- other 'craft' items
- books
- art supplies.

Generally speaking the way these businesses are run is that you hire either a cabinet or a space somewhere in the main shop where you display your goods, for which you pay either a weekly or monthly rent. These type of shops have what's often referred to as 'easy-in easy-out' terms, which means there are no tiresome leases to deal with. You can rent your space for anything from a month to a year or beyond.

You may be required to work in the shop one day a week where you will be responsible for selling other retailers' goods as well as your own. Weekends are usually the busiest times in these types of businesses and you would do well do run your own stand/stall during these periods even though it may not be your turn.

The retailers that I know who rent spaces usually rent a number of them in businesses across the country, so achieving lots of exposure for their goods.

Advantages to renting a small space
- Rents are usually fairly low.
- It is easy to get in and out.
- They can be profitable with the right goods.
- You can use your space as a marketing tool for your business. For example, you can have a display area where people can take your brochure or card and order your products online.

Disadvantages of renting a small space
- It can be time consuming.
- You often get more curious browsers than real buyers.
- You can suffer from theft.
- It is unsuitable for many businesses.

Nevertheless it's still an option worth considering.

Concession in a retail area

An excellent way of selling your products is to take a concession either in a shopping centre with a mobile kiosk or in another retail business.

For example many garden centres sublet some of their sales areas to businesses which complement theirs while not competing with them. These businesses include bespoke garden furniture companies, pet shops, camping and accessories shops, fish shops, fencing businesses, cycle shops and so on.

The advantages of basing your business at an already an established retail outlet is that you benefit from immediate trade as the garden centre will already have an established and loyal customer base that you can sell to.

Another considerable benefit to your business is car parking. Garden centres tend to be based outside town and city centres and usually have acres of parking available and not a traffic warden to be seen.

◆ TIP ◆

If your goods are heavy or bulky your customers will appreciate not having the headache of stopping outside a high street shop where there is no parking and every likelihood of getting a ticket.

Some shopping centres will allow you to rent a space in their malls where you can set up a temporary display or cart to sell from. Again the main advantage here is you'll have an instant customer base and won't have to shell out on advertisements telling everyone where you are.

One drawback of taking on a concession is that it can be relatively expensive. However I think that instant savings on things like business rates, insurance, water rates, advertising etc, combined with the fact that you will have access to a large and ready-made customer base, can make this a very worthwhile option.

Direct marketing

Another thing to consider is whether or not your products could be sold by direct marketing techniques. By this I mean purchasing specialist mail order lists and then writing direct to your target market. Most people will describe this as 'junk mail' but if used correctly, targeted mail shots can bring about immediate, impressive results. If you don't believe me then over the next few weeks start taking a closer look at your junk mail. You'll see that it comes from some very credible businesses such as banks, insurance companies, shops, clothes companies etc.

If it wasn't worth doing do you think these highly successful businesses would bother?

How to run your own direct marketing campaign

You will need to obtain an up-to-date mailing list that you can work from. Several marketing companies specialise in selling mailing lists and their advertisements can usually be found in the classified section of *Exchange and Mart* and by searching on the Internet.

Most companies will offer a service where you can buy a printed mailing list or pre-printed mailing list labels with the names and addresses already on. Although you can save yourself a considerable amount of time by purchasing pre-printed labels there is a big disadvantage to doing this. Remember that your business will not be the only business to have purchased this mailing list, which may mean that your target market becomes familiar, and understandably fatigued, with seeing the same label. So my advice is to purchase the list and then either make up your own labels or if your handwriting is up to it (handwritten envelopes get more attention that printed ones) handwrite all the envelopes.

Before purchasing a mailing list make sure:

◆ **You are buying from a reputable source.** If you can't see any client testimonials either on the marketing company's brochure or website they're probably best avoided.

◆ **The list is up to date.** The cheaper the list the more out of date it is likely to be. Ask the company representative to explain not only how they compile their lists but also how up to date they are.

◆ **Quantities.** You will need to buy in sufficiently large quantities to make your campaign work. Depending on what you're selling you can expect a positive reply of approximately 1 per cent. Thus if you're sending out 1,000 letters you can expect 10 positive replies.

Lots of books have been written about direct marketing and if you are thinking of using this marketing technique for your business I would recommend you do further research before buying any lists.

Although it can be expensive to run a direct marketing campaign it can be well worth it.

Exhibition or trade fair

Exhibitions and trade fairs can be great places to promote your business.

Exhibitions and shows

Exhibitions are usually open to the public and vary in size. For example, both the London and Southampton annual boat shows attract thousands of potential customers while a local plant or stamp fair may attract far less. However, the potential suitability of a show should not be judged solely on how many visitors it attracts. The most important thing to get right is to make sure that the show is attracting your target market.

Trade fairs

Trade fairs differ to shows in that they are only open to the trade. For example there are gardening trade fairs where everything from plants to the latest garden machinery are exhibited. If you're looking for agents to sell your products then a trade fair is the place to find them. Even if your products are unsuitable to exhibit, trade fairs are an important way of keeping up to date with what's going on in the market where you'll be operating.

Where can you find them?

There are literally hundreds of exhibitions and trade fairs going on throughout the year. The Internet is a great place to find out what's happening, as is your favourite hobby magazine. If you're really stuck to find an exhibition then phone up one of the distributors or manufacturers of a product you buy and ask them they know of any trade fairs or exhibitions.

Getting your own stand

One of the disadvantages of exhibiting at one of the major shows is that because they are so successful it's usually difficult to get a stand and once you get it, it can be very expensive. Smaller shows usually don't fill up as quickly and it's not too costly to rent a stand.

Depending on what you're selling, exhibitions and trade fairs can offer excellent potential. I know of a number of small, independent boat builders who exhibit at two annual boat shows and fill their order books for the following year, which justifies the relatively high price of having a stand there. I also know of other businesses who simply sell their relatively inexpensive cleaning products at these shows and also make sufficient sales to cover their rent, staffing costs and return a healthy profit.

Hotel foyer

Depending on your products, hotel foyers can offer excellent potential for a variety of hobby businesses where you can sell souvenirs, crystals, pictures, paintings, craft items, local walking excursions, cycle hire, tours etc.

◆ **TIP** ◆

The advantage of having your business based in a hotel foyer is that you have an instant shop without all the usual additional business costs such as business rates.

How to set it up

◆ Draw up a list of potentially suitable hotels in your area. You're looking for busy, quality hotels which enjoy all-year-round trade and have enough space in their foyer to site your display cabinet and desk.

- Go through your list and identify the hotel that you would most like to trade from and then the next one and so on until you have a numbered list.

- Find out the name of the manager and whether or not the hotel is part of a chain of hotels, and if it is the details of their head office. Do not mention at this time what you are looking to do. You're only concerned with getting contact details.

- Draft a suitable query letter, which must highlight the benefits to the hotel of agreeing to allow you have a concession in their foyer. Remember you must offer them some powerful benefits, for example, 'Your guests will appreciate being able to view our superior locally-crafted gifts, many of which are not available in the local shops.'

- Suggest either paying them a rent or commission on your turnover.

- Initially write to the top three hotels on your list. If these are part of a hotel group then you will need to write to the group's chief executive in the first instance. Say that you will phone in the next few days just to make sure they have received your letter and answer any initial questions they may have.

- Make your follow-up phone calls and try to gauge whether or not the initial hotels are interested.

Train station platform

Station platforms are also worth considering as a potential location for your business. Much will depend on what you're selling as to how suitable a railway station would be as a location.

♦ TIP ♦

One of the advantages of being based at a busy railway station is the sheer volume of pedestrian traffic that passes through each day.

There are a number of ways you could approach setting up your business. You could either rent an existing kiosk from the railway company, provided of course they have one free, or alternatively you could buy one or have it built.

How to go about getting a site

First find a railway station that would be suitable. If there is already a trader running the type of business you're proposing it's unlikely that your offer would be entertained. For example, most train companies are awash with offers from entrepreneurs to set up food and café businesses. When I spoke to a representative from one of the large train companies she told me that there would be little point in anyone trying to get a catering concession on their busiest platforms as there were already too many. She did go on to say that they would always be pleased to hear from anyone with ideas other than food and drinks.

Once you've identified a potential station then all you have to do is find out which company has the franchise for operating the platform and get in contact with their head office.

Café, shop or kiosk

If your business involves creating your own paintings, pictures, crafts, guide books etc, then as well as marketing them online you could also offer them on a sale-or-return basis to local cafés, shops and kiosks.

Getting others to market your goods in return for a commission is the oldest, and probably most reliable way, of building up your sales. Greetings card manufacturers are masters of this form of marketing.

How it works

+ Put together a selection of your products and work how much commission you could comfortably afford to pay someone for selling them on your behalf.

+ Draw up a list of prospective retailers. The reason for working to a pre-prepared list is that in the event you get a hostile reaction from one retailer you won't be put off. Instead you can simply cross their name off your list and continue with the next. Working with a list gives a more targeted approach.

+ Prepare a price list for your products. Try to make it as easy to read and attractive as possible, and either print or photocopy enough lists to cover all your prospective retailers plus some spare ones.

◆ Set aside some time to visit all your prospects. The most productive way is to set specific goals. Instead of simply saying that you'll visit all these shops in the next few weeks, set aside a few days and devote this time entirely to visiting your prospects. Not only is it much easier as you will get into a regular sales routine, but also more effective because you're less likely to leave it on the to do list.

Making your presentation

If you haven't already done this sort of selling it can be somewhat daunting. However it is also very easy because you're not actually selling anything – you're giving your customers a way of earning additional sources of income, a powerful benefit!

Generally speaking you will have to make your presentation by cold calling your prospects. I'd advise you don't try to phone and make an appointment as it's unlikely they'll agree to one. Retailers are used to representatives cold calling and most will tell you fairly quickly whether or not they're interested. If they're not, fine. Don't dwell on the rejection, just get on with working through your list.

When you walk into a card shop, café or kiosk, ask to speak to the manager. (The manager may of course be the business owner who may actually be the one you're already talking to.) As soon as you meet the manager/owner introduce yourself. Say that as a local artist/ photographer/craftsperson you'd like to offer them the opportunity to sell your products to their customers on a sale-or-return basis.

It's important you use the SOR (sale or return) method – this is standard practice for selling such things as cards, photos, paintings, guide books etc. Obviously if you can get your retailer to purchase a quantity of your goods then great, but a more likely starting point is for you to get your goods on display.

The benefit to the retailer is that there is absolutely no outlay on additional stock. The benefit to your business is you now have a retail outlet from which to sell your goods without having to pay large overheads. All you pay is commission.

How much commission should you offer?

This will depend on your product but most retailers will expect somewhere around the 30 per cent margin. Some will settle for less and others might want more so be prepared to negotiate.

Be careful of offering different commission deals to retailers, as if one finds out that you've offered a better deal to another you'll lose that account. Although many retailers compete with each other much of this is done on a friendly basis with many traders knowing each other. When something new comes on the market it's likely to get discussed and the first topic will be how much they can earn from it. If you find when making your presentation that one retailer will only accept your products on the basis of getting an unreasonable commission, then politely walk away.

When leaving your products you will also need to leave a copy of your stock sheet recording:

♦ an individual description of each product;
♦ retail price of each product;
♦ quantity of products left;
♦ date you'll be calling to restock and take your money.

Collecting your money and restocking

You'll need to work out a cycle of when to go and restock your product and collect what's owing to you. All you have to do is check what stock is left against your original list.

As you work through your round you will find that some retailers will already have done a stocktake and have either a cheque or cash ready for you, while others will be in state of complete chaos and might even say they can't pay you today as they haven't enough money in the till or some other excuse, which is why it's so important to have the agreed date entered on your original stock sheet.

What to do if they don't pay

It's important to have a pre-agreed date so that if you have problems you can remind them that you did check with them to make sure it was a convenient date to return. Don't get angry or demanding as there may actually be a genuine reason why the retailer can't pay you. Prior to your arrival he might have had to pay an unexpected bill or has simply had a poor week's sales takings.

My advice would be to check your stock and replenish where necessary and then agree another date to return. If after this date you're still having problems then you'd be wise to pull out and cut your losses. If the amount that you are owed is large then you should seek to recover your money via the small claims court or by employing a specialist debt recovery firm.

A word on merchandising

One of the biggest problems about using this method is that you will not be the only business competing for space in other people's retail outlets. There will be lots of other companies vying for floor and shelf space who will employ all sorts of techniques to make sure their goods are the most prominently displayed. Don't be surprised if you return after your first month to find you cannot locate your products at all. It won't be the retailer's fault, it will be because other companies employ merchandisers whose job it is to make sure their products stay at the front and others as much out of sight as possible.

If this is happening to you and your sales are suffering then it's time to start your own proactive merchandising. Hopefully the locations you've chosen aren't too far from where you live and you can pay regular visits to your retail outlets. If other merchandisers push your products to the back, you do likewise to theirs bringing your products to the front. As you live locally you will be able visit more regularly and thus win the battle. It'll soon become apparent to the competition that if they touch your display you will return to put it right.

Consider providing your own display stands

It might be worth your while investing in display stands for your products. Certainly this will open up the potential of even more retail outlets who otherwise wouldn't be able to display your products owning to lack of shelf space. Check the Internet for suitable suppliers and make up some advertising logos to go with them.

Boot fairs and market stalls

Although I'm not a great fan of boot fairs, they are nevertheless an excellent outlet worth considering to sell your products from.

Just like any other outlet or venue you will have to do your research prior to committing to setting up your stall or stand. The best way to tackle this is to visit as many boot fairs in your area as you possibly can. Remember that most of them will be on at the same time, usually Saturday/Sunday mornings. So allow yourself plenty time for your research. Assess each one and make sure you look closely at the people who are walking around. Ask yourself if these people are going to be interested in what you're selling. If they are, great. You've got yourself a relatively inexpensive part-time outlet for your business. If you think your products or produce aren't suitable then don't despair. Check out all the other boot fairs in your area and don't overlook the indoor markets.

Shop

Before deciding on a shop you need to consider carefully the costs involved, which go beyond rent. You'll have to consider business rates, insurance, maintenance, heating and lighting as well as other additional costs.

Leasehold or freehold

Just like buying a house or a flat, there are both leasehold and freehold retail properties available. With freehold property you own the building as well as the land it sits on and have full rights over the property and can sell it (subject to any mortgage conditions) whenever you wish.

You're also free, subject to planning regulations to make any alterations to the building. The disadvantages to buying a freehold property is that it is relatively expensive and can be very difficult to sell in the future.

With a leasehold property you purchase the right to use the property for an agreed period of time and are bound by the conditions of the lease. Most leases will require you to maintain the property at your expense; pay either a monthly, quarterly or annual rent payment; insure the building against damage, fire etc.

Whether your property is leasehold or freehold you will also be required to pay business rates. You will also have to pay to have the property surveyed and the solicitor's fees for the new lease. It's also common in the case of a leasehold property (not that you have to agree to it) for the landlord to put it as part of the contract that you pay all their 'reasonable legal costs' in negotiating the new lease.

Questions you need to ask yourself before deciding on a property

◆ **Location.** Is the shop located in an area where my target market is?

◆ **History.** What's the shop's history? What was the previous tenant's business? Have they relocated close by or gone out of business?

◆ **Crime.** Is the area prone to vandalism, burglary and does it become a virtual no-go area at night? How close is it to pubs, clubs and late night takeaways?

◆ **Size.** Look at size from the long term. What's the possibility of expanding your business? Be realistic here; some shops are about the size of your average ensuite. Can you really fit everything in? Forget about the great rent for a minute and look at it objectively.

◆ **Area.** You should always pay particular attention to what's happening in the area local to your business. Is it on the up with new businesses coming in? What are the plans for new housing? Is there already a business similar to the one you're planning to start?

◆ **Above and beside**. What sort of accommodation exists above and alongside your proposed shop? Most high street shops have some sort of accommodation above them which often is rented out, which isn't a problem if the tenants are OK. But what if they're not? How would that impact on your business?

Don't forget to check out your landlord

As well as researching the market local to where you're planning to open your shop, you should also find out as much as you can about your future landlord. Don't be shy about this. Remember that when you make an offer to lease a shop you will be asked for references and there will be background checks, credit checks and deposits to pay, while you will be provided with no information whatsoever about who your landlord is.

Purchasing a freehold property

The obvious advantage to purchasing a freehold property is that you won't have to pay rent. However, unless you're sitting on a pile of cash it's likely that you will need some sort of finance to fund your purchase. Commercial mortgages are available in exactly the same way as you'd get a mortgage to buy a private house. You could of course find a property which has a shop with accommodation over it so you can live above your business or rent the accommodation out as additional income.

Purchasing a freehold property is a drastic move for someone setting up their first business. If you have the sort of money needed to purchase a freehold shop then you're better off buying an established profitable business. This way at least you substantially reduce the risk and your money starts working for you from day one.

How do you find shops that are available to let?

There are number of ways including:

◆ walking through suitable areas looking for agents' 'to let' boards;

◆ contacting commercial property agents and asking them to put you on their mailing lists;

- checking on websites such as *Business for Sale* and *Daltons Business* for which a relatively small fee may have to be paid. (http://www.businessfor sale.com, and http://www.daltonsbusiness.co.uk.)

My final advice on taking on a shop lease, as opposed to buying a successful business that's already established and profitable, is to think very carefully before going ahead.

◆ TIP ◆

A lease agreement is legally binding and even if you cease trading after your first few months you will still be liable to pay all outstanding rents for the duration of the lease period you entered into.

Local authority concessions

Your local council may provide the solution of where to base your business. For example, the property from which one of our cycle hire businesses is based is rented from our local council. Prior to us getting this property we had searched in vain for somewhere suitable.

The main problem we faced was that we couldn't afford the high rents being demanded by local landlords. And the few properties that we could afford were in all the wrong locations. Then by chance we came across a derelict, disused seafront kiosk. It took a while for us to find out who owned the kiosk. Once we'd established it was the council we found out what was involved in trying to secure a tenancy.

What's involved in taking on a local authority concession

Depending where you live, your local authority may provide concessions for:

- fast food outlets
- crazy golf
- cycle hire
- boat hire
- beach goods
- cafés.

There are a number of way of obtaining a concession:

◆ Bid on an existing tender when it comes up for renewal.
◆ Purchase an existing concession.
◆ Suggest a concession by putting together a proposal.

Bid on an existing concession

The law requires your local authority to offer all concessions for tender once the original concession period has come to an end.

Usually these concessions are advertised in your local newspaper under the public notices section. You can also contact your local council and ask to speak to the concession officer who may be able to give you some indication of what will be coming up for public tender.

Most concessions work on the following basis:

1. The concession is advertised under the public notice section of one or a number of local papers inviting interested parties to make a written request for an information pack.

2. Information packs and tender documents are then sent out. The pack contains information on the concession that is being offered, including any special requirements.

   For example, if it is a boating hire concession there may be stipulations that you must supply your own boats, undertake all maintenance of the lake etc.

   You will also be informed of the date by which the council must receive your written tender bid. If your bid is received after this date it will not be considered.

3. Tender requirements will vary on the concession being offered but most will require you to confirm what rent figure you would pay were you awarded the concession together with other relevant information such as what experience you have in running this type of business etc.

4. Tenders are sent in using a pre-addressed envelope clearly marked for the attention of the officers who will be deciding on who to award them.

5. The envelopes are all opened by at least two council officers and a decision made. This decision is then placed before the relevant council committee for final approval and the successful party is notified.

It's worth knowing that the council are under no obligation to award the concession to the party who bids the highest rent figure. The final decision will be made on number of factors including:

◆ **Performance of the previous tenant** and whether or not they are bidding. If the previous concession holder has managed the business professionally and given a good service to the public it is likely that the council will look favourably on their application as they have proved their capability.

◆ **Experience of running the type of business** that is on offer. Again if someone can demonstrate a particular expertise the council will naturally be more inclined to take their offer more seriously than someone with no experience.

◆ **The rent being offered**. Councils have a duty to the public to ensure that they are getting the best possible return on their concessions, which means that although they don't have to accept the highest bidder, they will have to explain their decision to the committee (made up of elected councillors) if they don't go with the highest bid.

Unless you're already running the concession you won't really know how much to offer in rent. But this shouldn't deter you as everyone else (apart from the existing concession holder) is in the same boat.

Purchase an existing concession
Every so often concessions come for sale. The advantages to purchasing an already up and running concession is that you will be able to see the trading figures, talk to the business owners and investigate locally how well the concession is doing before investing you money.

A disadvantage is that even though you have purchased the business you will still have to submit a tender in the same way as everyone else when your concession term runs out.

Probably the most important question you want answered when considering whether or not to buy an existing concession is to find out why the business is up for sale. It's a good idea to do your own research in addition to the reasons given in any sales particulars. It may be up for sale because the local authority is unhappy with the way it has been run. If this the case do you really want to buy something that already has a poor relationship with the landlords?

As with purchasing any business, you should always employ professional help including a solicitor and an accountant. You will also need to have 'due diligence' undertaken which can be organised by your accountant. Due diligence is a legal term which means having the books and trading claims made by the current owner checked. You also need to check with the local authority that they have granted their permission for the business to be sold.

Suggest a concession

Another way to get a council concession, as we did with our cycle hire business, is to suggest your idea to the council. Provided they have suitable premises or a space available then you're halfway there. All you need to do is convince the council that the business you are proposing would be of benefit to the public and hopefully improve the area.

To suggest a concession:

- If possible identify a suitable vacant council-owned property or piece of land where you would like to base your business.

- Have a clear idea of the type of business you are proposing to run. In our case this was cycle hire and even if we didn't get a council concession we still planned to go ahead with our venture. So when we came to meet the officers from the council we knew exactly the type of business we were going to set up and were confident with our business plan.

◆ The council won't be particularly interested in what's in it for you – they'll want to know how the wider community will benefit from your proposed business. Therefore make sure you have at least two powerful 'what's in it for them' benefits before you make your initial approach.

Be patient

The key to working on any project that involves the council is to be prepared for sometimes unexplained and lengthy delays. So you must be patient. Getting irate and impatient will not do your cause any good. In my experience the people you will be dealing with – the council's concession officers – will be just as eager as you to see your business up and running and benefitting the local community. However councils are political to the point of tediousness, which means that in all probability everyone from the person who replenishes the loo rolls to the chief executive will probably have to be consulted on your proposal before any go-ahead can be given.

Be flexible

In the event that your proposal is turned down don't be afraid to ask why. It may be that you can revise your proposal and resubmit it so that it fits in more with the council's ethos and requirements.

Don't give up

This is true with everything you do. Sometimes it's easier to give up than put in that revised submission or tweak your idea so it fits into the council's greater scheme of things. Whenever you're tempted to give up, take a small break and clear your head of negative thoughts, get on your bike and go for it again. The things that are really worth getting in this life are often those which we have to fight hardest to achieve.

Why do businesses come up for sale?

It's a common misconception that the only reason businesses come up for sale is because they are doing badly. Certainly some businesses will be selling for this reason, but by no means all. Retirement and ill-health force many otherwise profitable businesses to be sold. I've read recently that many successful family businesses are being sold because no one in the family wants to take them over. So there can be a whole range of reasons for businesses coming on the market.

> Remember: if you are considering buying a business you should take professional and impartial advice before making any decisions.

SUMMARY

1. When deciding where to sell your goods and services from remember there are lots of options available to you.

2. Hiring space in another business's retail unit is an excellent way of keeping your costs down and making your venture more financially viable.

3. There are times when it will be more cost effective to buy an existing business than start your own. Don't be afraid to investigate these possibilities.

4. Many local authorities offer retail concessions, which can offer attractive prospects in terms of low rents and prominent positions.

5. Beware of shark landlords. Most property leases that you will be offered require you to upkeep and maintain someone else's business. Never underestimate how much this could cost you. Could your business support maintaining a property as well as returning a profit?

6. A high street shop isn't the only option available to you. Look for other low-cost opportunities.

8

Your Business on the World Wide Web

The Internet offers unlimited potential for KTEs.

Undoubtedly, the greatest single improvement to the fortunes of the Kitchen Table Entrepreneur has been the arrival of the Internet.

Where else can you launch a worldwide business for less than the price of a month's advertising in your favourite hobby magazine?

But despite the opportunities, the Internet is awash with global business failures.

There are any number of reasons for this, but lurking somewhere will either be one or a combination of these factors:

- Complete lack of understanding on the part of the business owner as to how the Internet works.

- Poorly-designed websites that make the business look amateurish and give the impression of being run from the entrepreneur's spare bedroom.

- Websites that are not designed to attract visitors to the site.

So what can you do to ensure that your website does what you want it to?

To answer this question you need to ask yourself **What's your objective in having a website?**

◆ Do you want a site that solely promotes your business and gives information about the services you offer?

◆ Or do you want a website that sells your products online?

◆ Or a combination of sales and promotion?

Before you go any further with your business website you need to be clear about your objectives.

Don't work under the misapprehension that simply because you have a website, visitors will come flocking to your site. The reality is that bringing customers to your website can be a full-time task. Once you get them there your website has to be absolutely right or they'll click their way out to your competitors.

Make no mistake about it – the Internet is cut-throat and there is no place for half-measures, poorly-designed web pages or sites that don't take credit cards.

There are three areas that you need to look at:

◆ Creating a website for your business.
◆ Marketing your website.
◆ Staying ahead of the competition.

CREATING A WEBSITE FOR YOUR BUSINESS

As I said earlier, before you go any further and even attempt to build your own site or commission someone to do it for you make sure that you have clearly identified your objective in having your own website. This is absolutely crucial to your future success.

For example, my businesses include a gardening business, cycle shop, boat hire, and home study course business. The objectives for each of my sites differs considerably.

My primary objective in having a site for the **gardening business** is to promote my main gardening business, which is maintenance and landscaping work.

So my site includes:

* details of the services we offer;
* reasons why someone should choose my business over my competition;
* testimonials from delighted customers who have used our service;
* gardener's diary;
* contact information;
* details of any special offers we're running;
* pictures of work that we have completed.

The site's primary objective is to get people to contact us as opposed to selling them anything. Therefore the success of the site can be gauged in how many enquiries we get through it. The process of turning those inquiries into actual orders is done offline when I go and visit prospective clients.

There are two objectives to the **cycle hire and sales business** website:

* to interest people in coming to our seaside location and hiring a bike;
* to sell cycles and accessories in our shop.

The objectives differ entirely from that of our gardening business, because not only do we want our website to be a marketing tool for our business, we also want to sell our products online.

The success of this site can be measured in how many new customers it brings to our cycle shop and hire kiosk, and how many bikes and accessories we actually sell.

Our primary objective with the **home study courses** site is to sell a range of innovative and inspirational gardening home study courses. The success of this site is ultimately gauged by the number of courses we actually sell. Selling on a site requires you first to get customers to your site, and then once there interest them enough in your course to make them enrol on one.

Write down now what is your site's main objective. Do this and you're halfway towards winning the battle!

Build your own website or employ someone?

When it comes to creating your own website you'll have to decide whether or not you want to create your own site or have someone build it for you.

Personally I prefer to build my own websites for the simple reason that I can update them whenever I like without having to pay fees to a web designer.

The main advantages to creating your own site are:

♦ that it is cheaper than employing a designer;

♦ that you retain control over your site and can move it to another server if necessary;

♦ that you have more control over bringing visitors to your site by adding guest books, free give-aways etc;

♦ that you can play around with your site until you get it right without having to pay a designer to do it.

The disadvantages are:

♦ unless you do it properly it can look amateurish and destroy your business's credibility;

- it can be time consuming;

- you need to know what you're doing and be computer literate.

The easiest way to build your own website

Sign up to a hosting company which offers template building
You can create a professional-looking site without having to have specialist knowledge. For example, most template websites are simply a matter of pointing at a menu and clicking the feature you want, then adding the text in the boxes.

There is an ever-growing number of companies offering these ready-made templates for your business, but you need to be careful as the quality of the templates can range from absolutely garbage to excellent. Most sites offer a free trial where you can sign up for 24 hours and try out the templates before committing yourself. It's well worth doing this.

Most of these sites also offer to register your chosen domain name for a small fee, which is often included in the price of the hosting. While undoubtedly this is a good idea, make sure that you do not get them to register your domain name until you are absolutely certain that you want to use their templates. Otherwise you may find they will charge you a fortune to transfer your domain name to another competitor.

◆ EXPERIENCE ◆

Both our Dutch cycle business and my own site www.paulpower.co.uk have been built using templates. My hosting company includes a shopping cart as part of the package and we can also accept credit cards.

Build your own site using software
If you have a basic knowledge of HTML or you already have web-building software, for example Dreamweaver or Microsoft FrontPage, you can either build your own site or purchase a ready-made template and then adjust this to suit your needs.

The disadvantage is that you will still need to pay a hosting company to host your site and you will also need to register your name.

My personal preference is to have it all with one company and then if either you need help or there is a problem you only have one company to contact.

Free website hosting and free template

There a number of companies that will allow you use their templates free of charge including hosting your site on one of their servers, but in return your site will either have to display their ads, or visitors will be bombarded with annoying pop-up ads.

My advice is that you should avoid these at all costs. Regardless of how hard you try you simply will not be able to encourage visitors to take your site seriously if their viewing is constantly interrupted by pop-up ads. Neither will you inspire confidence and credibility.

Have a page on an online directory

This is where you buy a page on another website's directory. I can see absolutely no advantage in doing this. The success of your site will depend on factors outside your direct control. You will have no control over the marketing of the parent directory site or have any influence over the direction it goes.

If you're just starting out I would suggest you join a hosting company where you pay a monthly fee for your site, which includes web page templates to get you started and allows you to add outside features like guest boards, newsletter sign-up scripts and so on.

Whatever you choose make sure:

- you can update your site content whenever you want and you are not charged for this;

- you can add features like guest books, e-zine subscription scripts, credit card processing and so on;

- the host site is reputable and you can see examples of other customers' sites. Most sites do this as a matter of course; if you don't see any email them with your request before you decide to sign up;

- there is no requirement for you to run others' advertising on your site;

- that you can include search engines 'meta tags' in your pages.

Designing your website

Always try to make your site interesting and unique, but remember your design should be appealing to visitors and search engines.

With an ever-increasing and bewildering amount of websites available in any particular area your site will have to be good enough to encourage visitors to come in and spend some time. We'll look at the various ways to make your site both interesting and interactive in just a moment, but first I want to introduce you to the two most important principles of good web design:

1. Your site must be search engine friendly.
2. It must be visitor friendly.

Search engine friendly

Make it your number one priority to make your site as search engine friendly as you can. To do this you will not only need to include key words in the main text of your site, but you'll also need to include key-word meta tags in your HTML coding.

There's nothing difficult about doing either of these things. If you've created your own site you can go to http://www.free-webmaster-tools.com/Meta-Tag-Generator.htm where their online software will generate free meta-tags for your website.

Try also to make your domain name relevant to what you're selling online as search engines also search under domain names. However, depending on the area that you're going to operate in, this isn't that easy as the obvious domain names will probably already be taken.

A good domain name will enhance your search engine ratings enormously.

Before adding key words to your site be careful that your site actually contains content relating to these key words. When search engine spiders, or worse still editors, visit your site they will be unlikely to list it if it doesn't bear any relation to your key words.

If, for example, you have a site selling camping gear and you include in your key words 'maps', 'guides', 'camping directories', 'camp sites', but your site doesn't actually contain any of these things you're in trouble. Not only are you running the risk of not being included anywhere by search engines, but equally importantly even if you are listed and visitors come to your site having searched under 'camping directories' they will rightly expect that this is, amongst other things, what you are offering. The chances of them staying in, let alone buying from a site that clearly isn't what it says it is, is highly unlikely.

When it comes to key words and meta-tags, honesty pays.

Visitor friendly

It's amazing how website owners think that visitors to their site want to be bombarded by music or other silly gimmicks like annoying things flying around the screen and getting in the way of seeing what the site has to offer.

If you're ever tempted to include music, remember this. Most work places in the country now have Internet access and I know from previous experience working in a large office that employees often spend time surfing the net when they should be doing other things. But what happens if your music blares out of their speakers?

Music and over-reliance on pop-up ads, gaudy colour schemes and poorly structured pages, will drive visitors away from your site in seconds. Once they're gone, that's it.

When coming up with a suitable design for your website try to keep it simple so that it's:

◆ easy to navigate, which includes providing a navigation bar on all your pages;

◆ easy to read – the colour of the text doesn't clash with the background colour of the page;

◆ free from large graphics that take time to download.

Spend time looking at as many websites as you can. Save the ones you like in your favourites folder. When you feel you have exhausted your search go back through them and start pruning your list. Strike off those that don't immediately grab you and then keep on going until you are left with about three or four websites that you really like, and build or model your own around their design.

I'm not suggesting you copy or mimic other people's sites but get your ideas for colour schemes and navigation structures from these. Surf any of the top search engines and you'll immediately notice that they all bear similarities to each other. This isn't because they are trying to clone their competitors' sites, but because certain colour schemes work better than others.

For example, how many times have you visited a website where the colour of the text clashes so much against the page's background colour that you can't read the writing? Or you visit a site, find what you want to buy but give up after many unsuccessful attempts trying to find how you buy it?

Employing a web designer

As I've said earlier, I personally prefer to build my own sites either using templates or website software such as Microsoft FrontPage. However there are certain businesses where the investment in hiring a company to design your website is well worth it.

If part or all of your business is going to involve taking online bookings, then you'd certainly benefit from a website where visitors can check availability and make and pay for their bookings online.

◆ **TIP** ◆

> The key to running any successful online business is to make it as easy as possible for your customers to spend their money on your site.

From the moment your visitor arrives at your site you want them to know that you're not only open for business, but here to help.

Imagine walking into to a high street travel agent and making an enquiry only to be told they'll get back to you sometime in the future. Whilst some people might go home and wait, most won't and will go into the next travel agent and book their holiday there.

It's the same online. One of the Internet's primary advantages is that everything is immediate. You can download brochures, prices lists, buy goods, book holidays and flights all at the click of a button. So if your business is going to be operating in these areas I recommend you consider employing a specialist.

Where do you find a designer?
I regularly get emails and telephone calls from companies trying to sell me web design. Occasionally I've been tempted to ask them to give me a quote and without exception I've been disappointed. Rather than offer bespoke web design packages they've offered to create up to six websites for me to choose from, which appear to be nothing other than cheap-looking, uninspiring website templates. When I've told them that I want to be able to update the content of my site regularly, they've given me a ridiculous price to do this.

By far the best way of finding a website designer for your business is to find a number of sites that you like the look of. Usually somewhere at the end of the home page will be a little logo or message saying who built the site. If there isn't one, send an email to the company saying how much you like their website and would they please let you have the details of the company who designed it.

But make sure that:

- you like the person who is going to be working on your site;

- you get a written estimate for your website package;

- you read a copy of the company's terms and conditions and you understand and are happy with them;

- you know how much the whole package will cost including hosting fees etc, and what will happen after your first year. Some companies may offer what appears to be a great deal in year one but will then charge you a fortune thereafter.

MARKETING YOUR WEBSITE

Creating your website is really the easiest part of setting up your online business. The hardest part, as with all businesses, is to get visitors through your doors, and once in, to buy from you.

Working on the assumption that you are going to be using your website both as a marketing tool for your business and a place where customers can buy your goods, you're going to have to work to a strategy if you are to succeed:

1. Bring visitors to your website.
2. Once they've arrived, get visitors to buy whatever it is you're selling.
3. Get them to come back again.

Getting visitors to your website

Obviously you're not going to be able to market or sell your products and services to anyone unless you actually get them to your site. There are a number of ways you can do this:

- upload your site to search engines
- list your site on specialist directories
- links
- webrings
- adwords at Google
- affiliate programmes
- contribute to other sites' newsletters and e-zines
- offline marketing techniques.

Search engines

One of the most frustrating things about search engines is that it can take a relatively long time before your site gets listed. My own experience has been that this can be anywhere between three to six months. Of course it may take you longer depending on your site and the market you are going to be operating in. However, I believe the wait is worth it and I also believe that given the time it might take to get your pages listed you should do this as soon as you can.

Regardless of any other technique you use to bring visitors to your site you must never ignore search engines. At the time of writing, search engines are still responsible for bringing the largest volumes of surfers to websites.

Search engines work on the principle that surfers type key words into their search fields and then the search engine suggests a list of potentially suitable sites.

While every search engine may have different criteria for listing sites, most will use ROBOTS, or spiders, to search the Internet for pages to list. Most will also have a facility on their home page where you can suggest a site for them to look at.

You can suggest your site by submitting your URL (Internet address). The advantage of doing it this way is that rather than waiting around for their BOTS or spiders to find your site, you're suggesting they come and visit. Even though most will visit your site it still takes time for your pages to get listed, if at all.

I mentioned earlier the importance of making sure that your site is as search engine friendly as possible and that your key words accurately reflect what your site is about. This is important as when the search engine's agents visit they will go through all the pages of your website and check to see whether or not your website actually is what it says it is before they'll consider listing you.

◆ TIP ◆

> Remember that search engines are businesses. The quality of their service relies on the accuracy of the sites they suggest when people put key words into their search fields, so it's essential the information they recommend is as accurate as possible.

Before submitting your site to search engines you should:

1. Make sure that your site is finished. This means no 'under construction' signs or 'coming soon' messages.

2. Draw up a list of all the search engines that you would like to have your site listed on. Obviously there are the main ones – Yahoo! and Google, but don't overlook the smaller engines and particularly any ones that relate to your hobby or interest.

3. Set aside some time and sit down and submit your URL to all the engines on your list. I've found doing this in one session to be far easier than on an ad-hoc basis.

4. Keep your list and check back at regular intervals to see whether your site's been listed. Remember it can take a long time before you get listed, sometimes as long as a year. Don't under any circumstances be tempted to keep re-submitting your URL until your site gets listed. Be patient and keep monitoring.

You'll often hear about companies claiming that they can ensure your site is uploaded to as many as 800 search engines. Of course they charge for this service and the costs can be high, plus there's no guarantee of what service engines you will be listed on.

Both your time and money would be better invested promoting your own site because your primary objective is to promote your site, whilst these companies' objective is to make profit from you.

The Internet is continuously changing so it's worth spending some time investigating further how search engines work and what you need to do to ensure your page is listed.

Specialist directories

Every hobby will have its own specialist directory website, many of which will be run by amateur enthusiasts as opposed to businesses. It's well worth getting a link on these sites and you'll find that most will include your site within a few weeks of you submitting your information.

The way to find the best directories is to use search engines. In the search field type in the sort of key words that you would expect that visitors coming to your site would use. The search engine will then suggest a number of sites and you should go through these and pick out any directory sites. Obviously if they're easy to find via search engine they're worth having your site listed on their directory.

Many will insist that you post a link from your site to theirs before they will consider listing you. If this is the requirement then make sure you do add their details in your links section before registering.

Links

Getting a link on the right website can result in visitors flocking to your site. I have had thousands of pounds worth of business from one website's links page.

Again what's needed here is a proactive approach, which means visiting as many sites as you can, compiling a list of these sites, and then contacting them asking them to place a link on their site. Your email request should include the fact that you'd be pleased to put a reciprocal link on your site.

The easiest way to find the best sites for links is to learn from your competitors. So if you haven't already, get a list of your competitors' URLs (website addresses). Then go to the search engine AltaVista, which is located at: http://www.altavista.com.

Once there you can find where your competitors are linking by entering link:competitorsdomainname.co.uk.

For example, let's say you're going to be selling kites and one of your main competitors is John's Classic Kites and their website address is www.johnsclassickites.co.uk. All you'd have to enter is links:www. johnsclassickites.co.uk. In a single search you will bring up all the sites your business should be linked to if at all possible.

The golden rule when it comes to asking another site to include your link is to read their links policy. Here they will tell you their submission policy, which could include that you must have a link on your site linking back to them before they will consider you. Or that you have to display one of their banners, or any one of a number of other things.

If you don't hear from them after a few weeks send them another polite email chasing them up.

Webrings

Webrings are ideal for hobby businesses because, unlike traditional search engines, webrings are usually run by enthusiasts for enthusiasts of a particular hobby or interest.

The advantages to promoting your site by joining a webring are:

♦ they cost nothing to join;

♦ provided your site fits in with the webrings genre, there's no reason why you won't be listed;

◆ some webrings will include you immediately or shortly after you join.

The first thing you need to do is identify which webrings would be suitable for your products or services. You may already know of a webring that might be suitable and if this is the case then all you have to do is send a request to the owner to join their ring. The webring owner will then visit your site to see whether or not it's suitable in terms of content, ethos etc. If it is you'll be accepted and sent some HTML code and graphics or banners that will you have to include on your site. As soon as this is done visitors to the ring will be able to visit your site.

The two main webring directories can be found at http://www.ringsurf.com and http://www.webring.com/rw. You can also search under key word 'webring' using search engines.

If you can't find a suitable webring for your site then you could start your own. To do this you can apply to Webring or Ringsurf or use any of the major search engines. As soon as you get another four websites to join your ring you will be listed in the main directories.

With the growth and popularity of the Internet I think you will find a number of rings suitable for you to join. If you don't, ask yourself why.

◆ **TIP** ◆

While not finding a suitable webring shouldn't stop you from going ahead with your business, it does suggest that maybe your business idea needs some more research.

Adwords at Google

At the time of writing the search engines Google and Yahoo! both offer businesses an opportunity to promote their website through an 'adword' scheme.

You bid on a certain amount of key words or phrases, that visitors might use to search for whatever it is you're selling. Which page your site gets listed on will depend on how much you bid.

For example in our Dutch bike business we could go to Google or Yahoo! and bid on the words 'Dutch bike'. Lets say we offer them 5p a word. This means that as soon as someone searches Google and enters the key words 'Dutch bike' they will at some point be presented with our site. And as soon as they enter our site through the search engine our account at Google will get debited by the amount we have bid on the word.

You open an account and then pre-pay an amount into it, which is then debited until either there is nothing left in your account or you pay more money in. How high your listing gets in the search engine will depend on whether you have been outbid on that particular key word.

Because if someone else is also selling Dutch bikes and they bid 10p on the same words their website details will be listed before ours.

The system has its advantages but the biggest drawback is that you are being charged for every visitor who comes to your site via this search engine, which mightn't be that cost effective. Nevertheless it's worth checking this scheme out to see if it is suitable for your business.

Affiliate programmes

Affiliate programmes operate on the basis that either you sell other businesses' goods and services from your website for which you earn a commission, or other websites sell your products and you pay them a commission.

Probably the most popular affiliate programme on the Internet is run by the giant online book retailer Amazon which has successfully run their affiliate scheme since 1996. You sell their goods from your website and earn a commission. This is how you do it:

1. Fill out an online application form to become an affiliate.

2. Amazon then visit your website and assess it for suitability and compatibility with their own goals and ethos.

3. If you are accepted you will be given special log on details and when you visit Amazon's website you can choose whatever goods you want to sell on your website.

4. You then cut and paste simple HTML code into your website, which displays whatever products you have chosen.

5. When visitors 'buy' from your website they will be automatically taken to Amazon's site where the sale, including processing of credit cards etc, takes place.

6. Each sale earns you a commission, which you can either take as an Amazon gift voucher or have paid into your account.

Most affiliate programmes work on this basis. There are all sorts of programmes that you can join from selling books to flights. Even the main DIY companies are now offering affiliate programmes.

 TIP ◆

> You will only earn commissions if your site already has customers coming to it. Joining a programme won't actually drive customers to your site, which is why it's well worth considering offering your own affiliate programmes.

There are two ways you can organise your own affiliate programme. Either offer your own programme by advertising it on your website and contacting other websites that you think might be interested in selling your goods and services. Or join one of the marketing companies which specialise in running affiliate programmes and for a fee they will recruit affiliates on your behalf and work out which one has sold what and to whom.

The advantages of working with a specialist marketing company are that your programme will gain immediate credibility which is something that can be difficult to achieve on your own. They also take away the headache of trying to work out which of your associates has sold what. Obviously the more products you offer through your site the harder this will be and the only reliable way of working out your affiliate sales is to purchase specialist software. This software could cost you anywhere from £200 to £20,000 depending on what you require.

At the time of writing http://www.affiliatewindow.com is probably the UK's largest affiliate management company. It's free to sign up to their website and browse all the affiliate programmes that you can apply to join. They also offer merchant schemes where they will, for a fee, manage your affiliate programme for you.

If you want to go it alone and purchase your own software or find out more about running your own schemes, the following websites should be useful:

◆ http://www.affiliatezone.com
◆ http://www.affiliateshop.com
◆ http://www.myaffiliateprogram.com.

Specialist companies come and go and it's always worth doing your own checks to find out the most up-to-date affiliate programmes and software tools. All you have to do is search the major search engines using key words 'affiliate programmes', 'affiliate software' or 'run your own affiliate programme'.

Contributing to other sites' newsletters and e-zines
As editor of my own online e-zine *Top Tips For Gardeners*, I'm always pleased when someone contacts me offering to write a short piece for the next issue. Provided their site is in keeping with what we're about I'm pleased to promote their website. Given that our e-zine has a loyal and ever-growing subscriber list the impact on those sites we promote can be very rewarding.

Even if you don't feel up to writing for another website's e-zine or newsletter you could contact the editor/webmaster and offer their readers an opportunity to enter a free prize draw. To do this they'll have to visit your site.

The power of newsletters and e-zines shouldn't be underestimated when promoting a new site. There are literally thousands of newsletters and e-zines published every second and the reason for their growing popularity is that subscribers benefit from reading the latest news and hot tips about whatever interests them and advertisers get to promote their website.

Many of the larger newsletters and e-zines now sell advertising space along the lines of a magazine or newspaper. Rates can be expensive and unless you've got something either unique or with worldwide appeal, I'd recommend you invest your time and energy in promoting your website in other ways.

Offline marketing techniques

As well as promoting your site online you should also consider some offline marketing, especially if your site has some sort of local appeal.

For example, our gardening business site has been set up primarily to promote our services in our immediate locality. Obviously there is a limit to how far we will travel and even though our site is up for the whole world to see, we're really only interested in promoting it locally.

Our offline marketing techniques include:

- **putting our website address on all our promotional literature** including business cards, brochures, posters, flyers and even on our T-shirts and fleeces;

- putting our **website address** on our company vehicles;

- having our **website address** as part of our letterhead;

- **a paragraph in every letter we write,** saying that if you want to see examples of our work and read what our customers say about us visit us online at www.paulpower.co.uk;

- **press releases and letters to the editor.** Writing to your hobby magazine and letting them know that you've just opened a new, specialist website is a great way of getting free publicity. If this doesn't work you can also write to the editors of newspapers and magazines asking if their readers would help you with your site by sending you their favourite tips or helping with someone other problem.

Part of our sales policy for our gardening business is that we don't pay for advertising. We run our own direct marketing using techniques we've perfected over the years we've been trading. But if we were to advertise, I'd include our website in every ad we run.

It's amazing how many companies don't include their website in their advertisements or even on their business cards. I'm always intrigued why they don't and whenever I ask it usually comes down to the same old problem – the website address is too long for the small advertisement.

This is one of the problems if you choose to host your website with a free hosting service. Rather than have a short, crisp, domain name you'll end up with something that no one will ever be able to remember and you won't be able to include in any of your publicity material.

◆ TIP ◆

Think carefully before deciding on a domain name. Choose one that people will remember, and that looks good on all your publicity.

STAYING AHEAD OF THE COMPETITION

As we've seen, getting visitors to your site is only one half of the battle. Now you've got them coming you want to ensure they're going to pay regular return visits.

If you advertise your business in your hobby magazine your potential customers receive a regular copy of their favourite magazine, either monthly or quarterly, and as soon as they see your advertisement are reminded of what you're offering.

This sort of continued exposure to your sales message is vital to stimulate sales. Experts believe that potential customers often need to see your sales message as many as five times before making a purchase.

If this is true it means that unless you encourage visitors to make regular repeat visits to your site you are losing out on an enormous amount of potential sales.

Encouraging visitors to return to your site

1. Ensure visitors bookmark your site.
2. Run regular competitions.
3. Provide tips of the day.
4. Offer free samples of your products.
5. Run your own newsletter or e-zine.
6. Create your own mailing lists.
7. Include an advice column.
8. Have a visitors' forum where issues can be debated and discussed.
9. Include a recommended links section.
10. Include job opportunities pages.
11. Have book reviews and product tests.

Ensure visitors bookmark your site

While some visitors will find your site through links on other websites, search engines and your ongoing marketing, many others will simply land there, not too sure how they got there. This sort of thing happens to me regularly where I'm looking for something, then follow links and more links and eventually find a really useful and interesting site. Then once I've left the site I've been unable to find it again. The solution is to bookmark it.

The way to get visitors to bookmark your site is to ask them! Of course to do this you need to offer them a benefit. For example let's imagine you're running a site for sailing enthusiasts. Visitors will need to see some immediate benefit to bookmarking your site. So if you say,

> This site is regularly updated with
> the industry's top sailing jobs.

> **Bookmark this site now** to make sure you
> don't miss out on the best opportunities.

You have a textbook marketing strategy, which is to offer a benefit followed by a call to action.

Don't only include an invitation to bookmark on your home page. Many visitors may reach your site in different ways. Include invitations and reminders to bookmark your site on a number of different pages.

Run regular competitions

Offering visitors the opportunity to win something from your site is not only a great way of getting them to return but it's also brilliant for getting them to sign up to your regular newsletter or e-zine. This way you can keep them stimulated with all the latest news from their favourite hobby as well as regularly exposing them to your sales message. (We'll look at what's involved in writing your own newsletter later.)

◆ **Prizes**: Make sure that the prize you're offering doesn't stop people from buying your products. For example if your top-selling item is a unique guide book and you offer this as a prize, you may find that a proportion of people who would otherwise have purchased your guide book will postpone this in the hope they'll win one. The best prizes to offer are those that don't compete with your own products and services but have some relevance to your visitors.

◆ **Benefit:** There must be some benefit to you to offering visitors the chance to win something. The most important benefit is to have people sign up to your regular newsletter so that you can keep in touch with them. Therefore make sure that in order to enter your competition they have to sign up to your newsletter.

◆ **Regular prizes:** Keep your site fresh by offering regular prizes so when visitors do return they can see the content has changed and the site will appear more alive and fresh.

Provide tips of the day

Hobby businesses are ideal platforms for providing tips of the day. I know of one model boat builder who subscribes to as many sites as he can just to get the tips. He's adamant that finding out about shortcuts is well worth it. And he also buys regularly from the sites which offer tips.

You can write your own tips, which can be one simple sentence or include more elaborate tips with drawings and pictures.

Don't forget also to encourage site visitors to submit their tips, which will not only reduce your workload but also make the site more sticky as visitors will get a buzz from seeing their tip online.

Create an archive where visitors can browse through previously published tips.

Offer free samples of your product

This won't suit every business, but if you can allow your visitors to sample or experience a free trial of your product or service it is an excellent way of both keeping people coming back to your site and getting new business.

Magazine publishers use this marketing technique all the time to sell subscriptions. They offer an initial free trial period of their magazine, after which you can either cancel your subscription or keep it going. It's a great way of generating instant customers. Who can refuse a free trial period?

Could this sort of marketing be used to promote your products or services online? Products which can be offered as free samples include:

- samples from guidebooks, recipe books, how-to style books etc;
- trial subscriptions to hobby magazines, newsletters etc;
- allowing visitors to advertise their own goods for sale free of charge on your website message board;
- free delivery on orders over a certain value.

The most important thing when running any sort of free giveaway or special offer is that it must have a sense of urgency. The best way to do this is to give your offer a cut-off date.

Take advantage of our free give away:
Book and pay for the walking holiday of your choice
before 31 March and we will give you two extra days completely free.

If you advertise that you regularly run free offers visitors will be encouraged to return to your site. A great way of making sure they do is offering them the opportunity to sign up for your regular newsletter where they'll be the first to hear about your free offers.

By getting visitors to sign up to your newsletter you'll be able to remind them that not only are you still around and offering terrific products and services, but also giving away some great offers.

Run your own newsletter or e-zine

The most important thing to remember when creating your e-zine or newsletter is that there must be a powerful benefit to get your visitors to subscribe to your listings. There's little point in saying 'Sign up for our free newsletter', as visitors won't bother. Most of us suffer from email overload and the last thing we want is yet more of it.

So make sure you offer a powerful benefit: 'Be the first to hear about our regular give-aways and special offers by signing up for our free newsletter.' Or just include the benefit in the title of the newsletter. For example, our gardening newsletter is called *Top Tips For Gardeners*, which in itself is a benefit.

I searched around for ages trying to think of a suitable title for our newsletter and eventually sat down and wrote down all the things I was going to include in my publication. When my list went on to several pages I began to realise that what I was planning to put together wasn't a newsletter, but a book! So I went back through my notes and scaled down what I was planning and found the only way I could really put together something useful and beneficial was to offer readers the benefit of my practical gardening experience in the form of tips. I've now built up a loyal readership who not only read my e-zine but also contribute to it by emailing me their tips.

Create your own mailing lists

Make it a habit to collect email addresses. Collect them when customers order your products, enquire about your products, pay for your products. Building your email contact list should be one of your primary and ongoing objectives.

◆ TIP ◆

Time your emails to fit in with the seasonal swings of your business.

If your business is selling walking holidays then send your e-zines to coincide with annual holidays, bank holidays and so on.

Another way to collect email addresses is to have a guest book on your site. Visitors have to sign up to your guest board before they can post messages. As part of their membership you can send them your regular e-zine, which of course they can opt out of at any time.

There are some people who should be on your list. To get the following people on your email list you will need to be proactive. If you wait until they join of their own accord it might never happen, so contact them and ask them if they would like to join. I've yet to have anyone say no.

1. Editor of your local paper.
2. Editor of your favourite hobby magazine/newsletter.
3. Your financiers, if you have any.
4. Your bank manager.
5. Your suppliers (suppliers will be better able to serve your needs if they know more about your business).
6. Managers of any professional/trade organisations that you belong to.

It's important to get these people on your e-zine circulation. Many, if not all, will be impressed that you've bothered to ask them. As well as increasing your businesses credibility, you are also building on existing relationships.

Setting up an automated newsletter

The greatest advantage of having an online business is that it never closes. Long after you've gone to bed for the night people can be browsing your products and services, and hopefully either requesting more information or buying online. Even though there's no one actually running your site, your site needs to be able to run on autopilot, which is why you need to use what is known as autoresponders.

Here's how they work.

Sign up to a site that offers an autoresponder service (see below). As soon as you become a member you can then cut and paste some codes into your site, which will create a visitor sign-up box on your web page.

The code can be customised so you can include your powerful benefit message to hook subscribers into signing up. As soon as visitors sign up you will be sent an email notifying you of this and the visitor will get an automatic email back from the autoresponder, but it will appear as if it's come from you. Again, you can customise your message to say whatever you want.

If you are offering a newsletter then say something like, 'Thanks very much for signing up for our newsletter; the next issue will be delivered to you shortly.'

Your visitor's email address is then automatically added to your subscription list and next time you write your newsletter you can send it using your autoresponder, which will email it to all those on your subscription lists.

An autoresponder is not just useful for sending out newsletters. You can use it for a whole range of marketing and sales devices.

Here are some other ways to use it.

◆ Instead of displaying your prices on your website you can invite your visitors to submit their email address using your text box link (autoresponder) promising them you'll email them a current up-to-date price list by return. You can send them a quick follow-up email a few days later asking them to contact you if they have any questions or would like to book. You can continue to send them emails (without overkill) at regular intervals announcing price increases etc.

◆ Use the autoresponder to send out free information. For example if you're running walking holidays you could invite readers to sign up to receive a free walking guide, which would then be automatically emailed to them. You could then set your autoresponder to send them a follow-up email in a few days time inviting them back to your site as you've now either updated the content, reduced prices, added new products etc.

◆ If your hobby business involves cooking, invite your visitors to sign up for some free recipes. Again your autoresponder could send these one at a time over how ever long a period you wish. This is a great way of building up client trust and allowing potential customers to get a taste of just how great your business is.

Used correctly autoresponders can send your sales rocketing, be careful you don't use them to the point of overkill or your customers will get so fed up they unsubscribe.

The most popular free autoresponders can be accessed when you sign up to http://www.freeautobot.com. The advantage to using this site is that you can pre-write a whole number of emails which will then be automatically sent at the times you pre-program. For example, your first email could be a complete price listing for your products followed up a few days later with a special offer if you buy today. This can be followed up a few weeks later, with another free offer.

I also like Constant Contact (http://constantcontact.com), which I believe is excellent for anyone wanting to publish their own e-zines or newsletters. This site has lots of brilliant features and your newsletters are made to look striking and professional. This site will offer to send your newsletters free to your first 50 subscribers after which you pay a nominal monthly fee. If you're really serious about setting up your own newsletter this site is definitely worth checking out. What I like most about this and Freeautobot is that your emails will not come with third party advertisements – something I believe you should avoid at all costs.

Lots of companies offer free web hosting and free autoresponders and it's tempting to sign up to them. All too late you realise that your emails or website are surrounded with all sorts of advertisements, which will do nothing for your credibility and will undoubtedly kill any off any chance you have of encouraging new business.

Include an advice column

The reason hobbies offer such great business potential is that at any given time there will always be newcomers to your particular interest and their quest for knowledge will be insatiable. By including a free advice column on your website you will encourage repeat visits, build up a loyal readership and get instant credibility as an expert in your field.

The following tips should help you run your own advice column.

- **It must free!** Don't be tempted to charge a membership to access the advice section. Rarely does this work and even if visitors do pay you to access this area of your site their expectations may well exceed what you're capable of offering and thus damage your main objectives – either to sell them a product or service or promote your business.

- **Make it interactive.** Even if you are an expert in your chosen field you should make your advice column more interactive by getting your visitors to post their questions and then inviting other visitors to answer them. The advantage of doing this is that you will attract more regular visitors who will want to give advice as well as simply reading your answers. You'll also find some engaging debates will take place as visitors disagree with one another's advice, making your site even more popular. Just make sure you include a disclaimer somewhere to the effect that you take no responsibility for the advice given and that this advice may not necessarily reflect your own views.

◆ **Keep an archive.** As your site grows in popularity and you get more and more material in your column break it down into sections and keep it in archives. This will allow visitors new to your site to search under different categories and make it easier to find the information they're looking for. It will also reduce the number of people posting repeated requests for advice that has already been discussed.

◆ **Monitor your column.** It's important to make sure that posters aren't being rude or aggressive to each other. Your aim is to provide a friendly, supportive advice column where visitors don't feel intimidated.

Have a visitors' forum
This is similar to the above. You can either just run an advice column or extend it to something a little more like allowing your visitors to post items for sale, items wanted, personal messages etc.

◆ TIP ◆

The more interactive and interesting you make your forum the more people will come back to it.

Again there are lots of companies that will provide you with a free visitors' forum board, which you can customise to knit into your own site. To find a suitable one search 'free forum board for your website' and go through the lists of sites offering this. Again make sure that visitors won't be beaten to death with free advertisements and annoying pop-ups every time they read or post a message.

Include a recommended links section

As well as actively encouraging your visitors to suggest suitable links for your site you should also search for your own sites to include. Draw up a list and contact them all asking whether or not they would like a free link on your site and in turn asking them if they would they put a reciprocal link to your site.

Whatever you do don't be tempted to charge people to put links on your site as this doesn't work.

Don't forget to make a list of your competitors' website addresses and find out where they are linked to, then approach these sites and ask them to add your site to their links.

Remember to check through your links regularly to make sure that they are all working and the sites they relate to are still relevant to what your site is offering.

Include job vacancies

Adding links to job vacancies on your site is always worth considering as so many people now use the Internet to search for a new job or career.

There are as number of ways you can do this:

- Include a situations vacant section on your visitors' forum.
- Search for interesting vacancies and post links to your site.
- Include a situations vacant column in your newsletter.

My favourite way is to include a round-up of interesting job vacancies in your newsletter. Do this and you're adding another powerful benefit for people to sign up to your newsletter.

All you have to do is spend a little time every month looking through your magazines and other websites and then include this information on your site and in your newsletter.

Have book reviews and product tests

If you're stuck for things to get your forum off the ground, you could create a number of sections including book reviews, product tests, price comparisons etc, and encourage your visitors to post their views.

What makes this worthwhile is that if someone posts a review of a well-known book or product the search engine robots and spiders may well index that page using the book or product title as a keyword, which could bring lots of visitors to your site that you wouldn't normally get.

HOW MUCH TIME DO YOU SPEND ON YOUR WEBSITE?

You may have come across Internet business opportunities where they conjure up the image that running one of these businesses only involves a few minutes of your time answering emails while your website does all the work.

Don't be fooled. Starting and running an online business takes just as much time as running any other business. Of course the main advantage of having an online business is that it's open when you're doing other things and reaches a greater and more diverse market place than any traditional shop.

You should spend as much time as you possibly can actively promoting your website and making sure that the content is interesting, fresh and appealing and that all working parts, guest books etc actually do work. We'll look in a moment at how you can run diagnostic checks on your website, but get into the habit of checking everything regularly. Particularly features like 'buy me now' buttons, shopping carts, online forms etc.

Get more out of your time:

◆ Set yourself daily, weekly and monthly goals and tasks.

◆ Every day, whether on or offline, do something to promote your site.

◆ Do what you say you will. If you promise visitors a weekly/monthly newsletter, then deliver on this promise.

♦ Monitor the volume of traffic to your site and try out different ways of increasing your traffic.

♦ Make sure the content pages are up to date and relevant. How many sites have you visited in the summer where the home page still has an autumn or winter theme?

Obviously you can save lots of time by making your website as automated as possible, but you will still need to promote your site making sure that you expose your business to the widest possible audience.

♦ TIP ♦

The more time you invest in developing and promoting your online business the greater the rewards.

I can't imagine you would want to spend anything less than a couple of hours a day, five days a week on your site until it really gets off the ground. Whenever you hear those Internet business gurus flannel on about days spent lazing on the beach or the golf course or sailing your yacht around the world, be very sceptical. Successful online businesses don't just happen – they are created and re-created until they achieve their goals to sell or promote your products and services online.

Is your site working as well as it could be?

If you have built your own site and are going it alone you must be absolutely sure that your website is running correctly. Some of things you need to consider are:

♦ **Browsers.** Although your website might look fine through your Internet browser this doesn't mean it will look ok on them all. Check how your site looks both through Internet Explorer and Netscape browsers.

♦ **Screen size.** Lots of people now use laptops and small screen monitors. How does your site look through a laptop screen or a small monitor? A common and easily made mistake is to create a site that fits wonderfully into your own cinema screen size monitor without making sure it'll fit into a comparatively tiny laptop screen.

◆ **Pictures.** A pet hate of mine is arriving at a website I'm interested in browsing only to find the pictures are so huge it seems to take forever for them to download. Make sure that your pictures, graphics, banners etc aren't slowing down your site. Where possible try to run your images through a software program where you can resize everything so it all downloads really quickly.

◆ **Music.** Beware of the consequences of adding music to your pages. The quality of the reproduction will depend on the speed of your visitor's Internet connection. Remember also that unless your site is actually music related most visitors will neither be impressed or encouraged to return if they're greeted with music on their arrival. If, and this is a big if, you must have music on your site make sure you allow your visitors to turn off the music and display your 'click here to turn the music off button' where everyone can see it.

As well as making your own checks you can also run some online tools, which will check that your HTML code, links etc are all in good working order. Some sites that offer this service include Site Inspector: http://www.siteinspector.com, and Net Mechanic: http://www.netmechanic.com/toolbox/html-code.htm.

Check to see if you're listed in the search engines
One of the most frustrating things about search engine submissions is that they won't tell you when and if your pages have been listed. The last thing you want to do is to keep re-submitting your site – do this and you run the risk of being accused of spamming and you'll never get listed.

An easy way to see if your site is listed is to go the search engine AltaVista (http://www.altavista.com). Once there check by entering the following in the search field: url:*yourdomainname*.co.uk/directory/page.html.

You will then be able to see where you are listed. As well as the above you can also go to any search engine and enter your domain name to see if any of your pages are listed.

Don't forget also to go the main search engines and use the key words that you would expect those looking for your site to use. For example, if you're running painting holidays in Wales, then go to Google or Yahoo! or one of the other main search engines and check to see what comes up.

As soon as you see a competitor's site write down their domain name and use the technique I showed you earlier to see who they are linked to, which is where you want to be also.

As I said earlier, there are a number of commercial sites who, for a relatively hefty fee, promise to submit your site to lots of search engines. They'll only *submit* your site to these search engines; there's no guarantee that your pages will get listed.

A number of sites that offer a submission service are listed below. You may find that the cost of purchasing their submission package is justified depending your site's objectives.

◆ Site Announce: http://www.siteannounce.com.
◆ Submit it: http://www.submit-it.com.
◆ Get Submitted (web hosting, marketing, site submission). http://www.getsubmitted.com.

Software and sites are changing all the time so play around with search fields using key words such as 'submit your site to search engines' etc.

Do you know who is visiting your site?
I like to know who is visiting our websites as not only does this help with determining how successful our promotional strategies are, but it also means we can then tailor our products and services to our visitors.

There are a number of ways you can find out more about your visitors. For example, your website host may provide you with a log report recording your site's activity, or you could add a tracking service to your site.

Extreme Tracking (http://www.extreme-dm.com) offer a free tracking service. All you have to do is register with the site and then follow the online instructions. They will give you some HTML code to paste into your pages and this will record your site's activity.

If your provider already supplies you with log files then you'll need to be able to interpret the data by subscribing to a web traffic analysis service, for example Analog: http://www.analog.cx.

EBAY

Ebay needs neither introduction or explanation. At the time of writing it is the world's largest online market place and a virtual Mecca for hobby enthusiasts.

Opportunities for hobby businesses

Ebay offers enormous opportunity for any collector both to sell and source their goods. Some collectors I know have shut their shops and now trade exclusively online while others have kept their shops, but vastly increased their sales by selling on ebay.

My own view is that not every business will suit ebay retailing. In fact in some cases selling your goods via their auction process may actually devalue your products as everyone bidding will expect to get them at a reduced price. For example I've noticed that the specialist Dutch bikes that we sell in our business seldom manage to achieve their reserve price.

However this hasn't stopped me from using ebay. We've purchase all sorts of bits and pieces at hugely reduced prices for our business. Because ebay works as an auction the effects of supply, or should I say over-supply, has both a dramatic and near instant effect on prices.

We have found ebay an excellent place to purchase:

- quality used and often near-new office equipment
- tools for our bike and gardening business
- low-cost packaging materials for our mail order business
- stationery packs
- accessories for our hire business
- memorabilia for use in our marketing campaigns.

Before we purchase anything for our business we now check on ebay. Doing this has not only saved us thousands of pounds but also made us far more conscious of how much we spend. Prior to ebay we wasted hours searching through catalogues checking for prices only to choose a supplier, contact them and then find out they were either out of stock or there had been a price increase.

Setting up and starting your business is probably going to cost you far more than you originally anticipated. Try to source all you can using ebay or similar auction sites.

I know of one mobile caterer who spent an absolute fortune on new catering equipment only to find that he didn't like the business he'd got into. When he went to sell his expensive equipment he found he could only get a fraction of what he'd originally paid for them. Why? Because the company that had sold him all this equipment sold 'business packages'. In other words they sold him a business idea. Buy one of our super-duper catering trailers and become the next McDonald's. Of course he wasn't alone and judging by the pages and pages of this sort of equipment that come up on ebay every week it's clear how many 'business opportunity seekers' didn't find this sort of business worked.

So if your goods and services aren't marketable on ebay, don't despair. It still an excellent place to save money.

SUMMARY

1. Every business should have an Internet presence.

2. Create the best website you possibly can. Remember your website is your virtual shop window. You should put as much thought and effort into creating your online image as you would if you were to open a high street shop.

3. Your site must be 'sticky' if it is to succeed. Not only will you need to encourage visitors to come to your site, but also to return regularly.

4. Ebay offers enormous potential for hobby businesses both in sourcing products for your business and opening and selling online.

9

The Mechanics of
Starting Your Business

I've deliberately left this chapter until last as I hope that by now you will not only have a greater idea of how your hobby can be turned into a successful business, but also what form your business will take.

Every business will be unique and have its own peculiarities. To provide all the information needed to start every business would be an impossible task and so I suggest you read what follows by way of an introductory guide to what's involved. It may be that you will have to research further to make sure that the business you're planning to start complies with all the rules and regulations of the day.

The first thing you will need to decide is which 'trading identity' is suitable for your business.

DECIDING ON A TRADING IDENTITY

There are a number of trading identities that you can choose from including:

- sole trader
- limited company
- partnership
- cooperative.

It's important to choose the most suitable trading identity for your business.

If you're in doubt what identity to start with you could start your business as a sole trader and then change to a partnership or company at a later date. Changing from a sole trader to a company is relatively easy. However changing from a company to a sole trader, although achievable, is much more difficult and can be expensive.

Only you can decided which one suits the type of business you are planning to start.

Sole trader

Sole trader is basically you trading as your business. For example Fiona's Flowers, or Greg's Hairdressers, or Paul Power Landscapes. It is the most popular choice of trading identity for those offering either a service or a small retail concession.

Some important advantages to trading as a sole trader

- **Easy to set up without any costs.** You simply trade as you are, eg Paul Power trading as Paul Power Landscapes.

- **Complete control over your business.** You are your business, which means you can retain complete control over all your business-making decisions without having to consult other directors, partners etc.

- **Easy to change to another trading identity.** It's far easier to change your trading identity from that of sole trader to a limited company. Going the other way, ie, limited company to sole trader, can be very expensive and bureaucratic.

◆ **Accounting.** Your trading accounts do not have to include a balance sheet such as you would have to provide for a company.

Some disadvantages

◆ **You are personally liable for all your businesses debts.** This liability is unlimited and should your business fail you could end up losing your personal assets such as your home, car, furniture etc.

◆ **Credibility.** While some businesses are suited to that of sole trader and customers like the idea of doing business with a person as opposed to a company, others do not. The travel business is one business where people need to be convinced that when they are paying their deposit and final holiday payments their money is being paid to a company and not an individual.

A sole trader is an ideal starting point for your business if you're simply selling something at craft fairs, exhibitions, through your own website, etc. It is also suitable for offering services, for example wedding planner, personal organiser, florist etc.

Remember that the main advantage to being a sole trader is that you can easily change to another trading identity as your business grows. My first business was Paul Power trading as Paul Power Landscapes – a sole trader – but this business is now run as a partnership.

Another advantage to you as either a sole trader or partnership is that in the event you make a loss you can deduct your losses from future profits, provided these profits are made from the same business. You can also deduct losses from other income you have gained either in the year you sustained the loss, or the previous year, including any personal income you might have.

How to set yourself up as a sole trader

Setting yourself up as sole trader is relatively straightforward.

1. Contact the Inland Revenue

Request the form that you need to complete to register as self-employed. You should do this as soon as you start. If you fail to do this within the first three months of becoming self-employed you risk a fine of £100.

The Inland Revenue also publishes a free *Starting Up In Business* guide, which is full of useful information regarding taxation and national insurance, employing people etc.

Contact the Inland Revenue either by phone (08459 15 45 15. Open Monday to Friday 8am to 8pm and 8am to 4pm on Saturday and Sunday) or online at www.inlandrevenue.gov.uk/startingup/. You can register and download copies of their guides.

2. Your business name

We looked at what's involved in choosing a name for your business in Chapter 3, but you need to be aware that if you are going to trade using a different name than your own, you must also include your own name on your headed note paper.

Therefore if you're a sole trader and name your business Discover Cornwall on Foot, somewhere on your headed notepaper you will have to include your name, trading as Discover Cornwall on Foot.

For example, if it was my business it would read: 'Paul Power trading as Discover Cornwall on Foot'.

3. National Insurance

You will also be required to pay flat-rate Class 2 National Insurance Contributions currently at £2.05 a week, which can be paid by direct debit.

If your profits exceed a certain limit, you will have to pay Class 4 National Insurance Contributions. The present limit is £4,745.

If the earnings from your business are low then you may not have to pay national insurance, but you must apply for exemption.

4. Staff

Sole traders are often incorrectly referred to as 'one-man bands'. However as a sole trader you can employ as many people as you need while still trading as a sole trader. The term sole trader refers to the business owner, and not those working in the business.

If you're planning to employ staff you will need to collect income tax and national insurance contributions and pay these to the Inland Revenue. Your employees will be paying tax on a PAYE basis, while you will remain paying tax on a self-employed basis.

4. Decide whether or not to register for VAT

If you decide to register for VAT you should inform Customs and Excise and register your business with them. We'll look at the factors that you'll need to consider when making your decision in just a moment.

5. Record keeping

You are required to keep an accurate and truthful record of all your business income and expenditure.

How you record these transactions is entirely a matter for you. If you wish to record them on a roll of toilet paper using a crayon, then you may. Of course it makes sense to record them in a format where you as the business owner can readily see at any given time whether your business is making a profit or loss.

Regardless of the business identity you choose, you will have to some form of bookkeeping procedures in your business. I'd recommend everyone read Peter Marshall's excellent book *Mastering Book-keeping, A step by step guide to the Principles and Practice of Business Accounting.* published by How To Books ISBN 1857038975.

6. Comply with any other regulations that may be applicable

Depending on the type of business you're going to start, you may have to register with other government agencies. For example if you're going to be preparing or selling food then you'll need to contact your local environmental health department and comply with any statutory regulations.

You're now ready to trade as a sole trader.

Partnership

This is a similar identity to that of a sole trader but there are two people instead of one.

The advantages are much the same as being a sole trader, however when it comes to making decisions you will obviously need to reach agreement with your partner.

Having a formal partnership agreement

Partnerships work well when things are going well but if things go wrong you will need something to fall back on. For example:

♦ one partner wants to sell the business and recoup their investment;

♦ one partner no longer wishes to work in the partnership but doesn't want to sell the business;

♦ additional cash is needed to expand the business but only one partner is able to the raise the cash.

With a partnership there are lots of 'what if's to consider. Even if your partner is your husband, wife, relative or best friend you should have a formal partnership agreement drawn up by a solicitor. Remember also that over time your partner's personal circumstances may change. You might start off as two carefree friends with lots of time to devote to your business and everything go well. Then either you or your partner marries, has children, and is no longer able to devote the same amount of time that they previously did to your business.

What happens when you one of you works fewer hours than the other and still wants the same return?

Or your partner's wife decides that she too would like to be a part of the business?

Or your partner gets divorced and their husband decides that they are entitled to a share of the business because they have been married to one of the partners?

Lots of questions need to be answered before entering a partnership, which is why you will need to have a deed of partnership drawn up.

Deed of partnership

A deed of partnership is a legally binding agreement between the partners of a business. This agreement describes how the partnership is to be run as well as detailing individual duties and obligations.

A deed of partnership will usually cover:

- the amount of money each partner is putting into the business
- profit-sharing agreements
- hours of work for each partner
- salaries
- future changes in the partnership – what happens if one partner dies, marries or wants to leave?

Business debts are joint

Just as a sole trader has unlimited liability for their business debts, partners have unlimited liability for their business debts, too. So if your partner accumulates business debts without your knowledge, you are also liable for them.

Can more than two people form a partnership?

Yes. A partnership can be for two or more people, however only those partners over the age of 18 are legally bound by the terms of any partnership agreement.

Partners are referred to as members of a partnership.

Can there be different types of partners?

Yes. There can be general partners, sleeping/dormant partners and even companies can be partners.

- **General partners.** A general partner is one who invests in the business, takes part in its running and shares in any losses or profits the business makes. Every partnership must have at least one general partner.

- **Sleeping partners.** Sleeping partners invest in the business and share in any profits or losses, but do not take any part in running the business.

  Sleeping partners are often friends or relatives who invest in new business ventures, for example putting up some capital to purchase a business, stock, premises etc.

  The important thing to note about sleeping partners is that although they do not take any part in running the business, they are still legally jointly responsible for any business debts and losses.

- **Companies.** Companies can be partners in another business. They share the same rights and responsibilities as other partners, however will be responsible for additional tax matters and reporting obligations.

Limited liability partnership

You can also form a limited liability partnership. To do this you will need to submit an Incorporation Document (Form LLP2) at Companies House.

The following information is required:

- Name of the limited liability partnership.

- Location and address of the limited liability partnership's registered office.

- Names and addresses and date of births of each member.

- Indication as to which of these members are the 'designated members'.

Designated members have certain duties, which include appointing an auditor, signing the accounts, delivering the accounts and annual return to Companies House and notifying them of changes to the members, registered office or name of the business.

With a limited liability partnership you are also required to display your business name, which must be the name of the limited liability partnership outside all your places of business and on all your notices.

Your company letterhead and order forms etc must show the place of registration, registration number, the fact that it is a limited liability partnership and the address of your registered office.

Taxation

You must contact the Inland Revenue and inform them that your new partnership exists. You'll then be sent a partnership return, which you must complete. This will include a partnership statement, which shows how profits and losses have been divided amongst the partners.

Although usually only one member of the partnership is nominated to complete the partnership return, every partner is liable in the event of any penalty if the form is submitted late, or there is a false declaration etc.

Similar to a sole trader, most partners will pay tax as a self-employed person, which means they will be responsible for paying their own national insurance contributions.

The procedure for a partner registering with the Inland Revenue is the same as for that as a sole trader.

Likewise if your partnership employs staff, you as employers are responsible for collecting your employee's tax and national insurance contributions on behalf of the Inland Revenue.

Setting up your business up as a company

The words 'business' and 'company' are often misunderstood. Basically if you're trading as either a sole trader or a partnership, you are a business, and if you have a company you will either have a public company or a limited company.

A public company

A public company will have PLC after its name.

To form a PLC you must have an authorised share capital of at least £50,000 of which at least one quarter must be paid on each share plus any premium. This means you would need a minimum of £12,500 (a quarter of £50,000) to form one.

Every public company must have two directors and a company secretary.

A private company

When you form a private company you do not need to have an authorised share capital of £50,000 to form your company.

Neither do you need to have two directors, but you do need to have a company secretary. If you have only one director this person cannot also act as company secretary. Therefore as a minimum you will need a director and company secretary.

The director and company secretary can be related, for example husband and wife.

Director's duties and responsibilities

Becoming a company director means that you accept certain duties and responsibilities, which include:

♦ Acting in good faith and in the interests of your company.

♦ Not using the company for any fraudulent purpose, which includes defrauding creditors or deceive shareholders.

♦ Never allowing the company to trade while insolvent. This is referred to as 'wrongful trading' and if you do so you may have to pay for any debts incurred by the company while insolvent.

- Complying with the requirements of the Companies Act.

- Having a regard for the interests of employees in general.

How to form a company

There are a number of options:

- Form the company yourself.
- Instruct an accountant or solicitor to do it for you.
- Purchase a ready-made company.

Forming your own company

Forming your own company can take several weeks and if at all possible you'd be well advised to employ either an accountant or solicitor to do it on your behalf, or purchase a ready-made company.

If you do decide to do it yourself you will need to get all the relevant documentation from Companies House by phoning and requesting a starter pack.

You will then need to register the company with the Registrar of Companies by sending in:

Memorandum of Association. This will include stating the name of the company, the location of the registered office and the objectives of the company.

The Registrar will need to approve the name of your company. In the event that another company is already using the name you choose for your company, you will have to come up with another name.

Articles of Association are the rules by which your company will be managed. You can either draw up your own articles, or if you don't the standard format set out in the Companies Act will be adopted.

Memorandums of Association and Articles of Association can be purchased from law stationers.

You will also need to complete the following forms:

Form 10. This is the form used to notify Companies House of the first directors and secretary and the location of your registered office.

Other details required include details of the company director's occupation, nationality and other directorships held within the last five years.

Form 12. This is a declaration of compliance.

Form 117. You must send this form in before the company starts trading.

Registration fees. There are two registration fees to choose from. You can either pay the standard fee of £20 or you can pay £80 if you want to use the same-day service.

Instructing a solicitor or accountant to do it for you. Fees charged by these professionals vary and it's worth shopping around to get the best quote. Not all solicitors will undertake company formations.

Purchasing a ready-made company. There are a number of businesses that specialise in selling off-the-shelf ready-made companies. These companies will, as the name suggests, be already formed and ready to trade complete with a company name. You can if you wish change the company name provided of course the name hasn't already been taken.

To change the company name you will need to:

◆ Convene either an annual general meeting or an extraordinary general meeting and pass a special resolution agreeing the new name.

◆ Send a signed copy of the resolution to Companies House together with a registration fee of £10, or £80 if you require same-day-service.

Businesses that sell ready-made companies can usually be found advertising in *Exchange and Mart* and on the Internet by searching under 'ready-made companies for sale'.

When buying an off-the-shelf company make sure that the price includes a certificate that the business has never traded. Otherwise you could find yourself buying a trading business and inheriting its debts.

Taxation

The important thing to remember when you choose to form a limited company is that you are going to be working for this company as opposed to being self-employed.

◆ You pay tax as an employed person on a PAYE basis.

◆ Your company also pays tax on its profits, due nine months after the end of the accounting year.

Other requirements

You are required to publicly display the Certificate of Incorporation and the registration date and you must also put the company name outside your office premises.

The following information must be shown on your company stationery:

◆ Full registered name of your company.

◆ Either the names of all company directors or none of them.

◆ Place of registration, eg Registered in England.

◆ The registered office address and the trading address of the company, indicating which is which.

◆ Company registration number.

The advantages of forming a company

There are a number of advantages of forming a company as opposed to trading as sole trader or partnership (except for a limited liability partnership).

The most obvious being that as a company director your liability for the company's debts is generally limited to your amount of shares. Your personal assets cannot be touched unless the company has been trading fraudulently or when the directors knew that it·was insolvent.

A possible disadvantage is that you are no longer self-employed and are in fact an employee of your company, albeit a director. This means that even though you have invested your money into your company, you can no longer treat it as your own. Your investment forms part of your company's assets and cannot be recouped as easily as if you were operating as a sole trader.

On the other hand if you are trading as a sole trader you are actually trading as yourself, which means you do own your business. There are no company regulations and legalities to follow if you want to sell some of your business assets or release some of your initial investment.

Cooperative

You could choose to run your business as a cooperative.

This form of trading identity would be best suited to a group of hobby enthusiasts wanting to set up their own business where the business assets are all owned by the workforce. Or if this is not possible immediately, then it must be the aim of the cooperative to own them eventually.

What makes a cooperative different from other businesses?

1. The management, business objectives and use of the assets must be controlled by the workforce.

2. The assets of the business must be owned by the workforce, or it this is not possible, it must be the aim of the cooperative to own them eventually.

3. The only reward for investing money for a cooperative can be interest on the loan. Any profits arising as a result of any investment should be shared amongst the workforce.

4. The cooperative should only be disbanded if all its members agree.

It's unlikely that a Kitchen Table Entrepreneur would choose to form a cooperative. However it's possible that a group of KTEs might want to form a cooperative to produce their own goods or services etc, such as a group of candle makers, craft workers, artists etc.

REGISTERING FOR VAT

At some point you will have to decide whether or not to register for VAT. I say decide because not all businesses will have to register. Before we get to look at the circumstances when you must register for VAT, let's look at VAT itself.

What is VAT?

Value Added Tax is an indirect tax on consumer expenditure collected by HM Customs and Excise. Most business transactions will involve either supplying goods or services or a combination of both.

The price charged to the consumer will have included in it an element of VAT unless the goods or services are VAT exempt. We'll look at exemptions in a moment, but basically there are three VAT rates, which are:

- standard rate – currently at 17.5 per cent
- reduced rate – currently at 5 per cent
- a zero rate.

These rates do not apply to all goods and services because some goods are what is know as VAT exempt, which means no VAT is payable. Also supplies that are outside the scope of VAT are those that are:

- made outside the UK and Isle of Man
- not made in the course of a business.

Items which are exempt from VAT
A full list of items that are exempt from VAT can be found by contacting Customs and Excise. The following is an indication of items exempt from VAT.

Where your business activity involves:

◆ providing credit
◆ insurance
◆ health care (with some exceptions)
◆ postal services
◆ most types of betting, gambling and lottery
◆ membership benefits provided by trade unions and professional bodies.

As you can see the chances of your providing goods and services that do not have to charge VAT are limited. Broadly speaking, a Kitchen Table Entrepreneur's business will attract VAT.

How does VAT work?
Let's take the following example.

I set up a business making homemade soaps. In order to do this I have to buy in raw materials from a wholesaler and I pay VAT on these items at 17.5 per cent.

I am registered for VAT. I can claim back the VAT that I have paid on these raw materials from HM Customs and Excise. The tax that I can claim back is what is known as 'input tax'. This is done by making what is known as a return to Customs and Excise.

However, I can only do this if my business is registered for VAT. Otherwise I cannot claim back the VAT.

Then as soon as I sell these goods to my customers I must charge VAT at 17.5 per cent. The VAT I charge my customers must then be given to HM Customs and Excise and is what is known as 'output tax'.

The mechanism by which you pay Customs and Excise is by completing *a return*. So my return to Customs and Excise will comprise of two taxes – output and input tax.

My soap making example might then look like this:

I buy my raw materials for £100 plus VAT at 17.5% giving a total of £117.50.

Therefore my input tax, ie the money I can claim back from HM Customs and Excise, is £17.50.

I then re-sell these goods to my customers for £150 plus VAT at 17.5% giving a total figure of £176.25.

Therefore my total output tax, ie the money I owe HM Customs and Excise is £26.25.

My return will then be as follows:

Total output tax	£26.25
Less total input tax	£17.50
Total owing	£ 8.75

In reality I may actually be able to claim back more input tax as I can claim back VAT on anything I have to buy to produce my final goods. Therefore if I have petrol expenses I can claim back the element of VAT included in petrol and so on.

I am unregistered for VAT. Here I simply buy my raw materials for £100 plus VAT = £117.50 and then sell them to my customer without having to charge VAT.

Cost of raw materials would be £117.50 because I cannot claim back the VAT, however I do not have to charge VAT on my finished product, which means that I do not have to add 17.5% VAT to the final price I charge my customer.

When must you register for VAT

As you can see there are advantages and disadvantages to registering for VAT. Lots of smaller business decide not to register for VAT as they believe it to be uneconomical.

Examples of this are guesthouses, many of whom choose to stay deliberately small and operate below what is known as the VAT threshold.

The VAT threshold

If the value of your taxable supplies is over a certain limit you must register for VAT. The limit at the time of writing is £60,000 per annum. The exception to this is if your supplies are wholly or mainly zero rated in which case you need to apply to HM Customs and Excise for an exemption.

Therefore if your business sells more than £60,000 per annum you must register for VAT, unless what you are selling is zero rated in which case you can apply for an exemption. This figure is usually subject to some form of change in the government's annual budget.

You can see now why certain businesses decide to run their business so they don't reach this ceiling.

Should I register for VAT if my turnover is less than the threshold?
Deciding to register your business for VAT will depend on a number factors. The important thing to know is that you don't have to apply for VAT registration immediately. You can apply at some future date. So don't feel you have to rush into this decision.

If you do decide to register for VAT you will have to be a 'business' in terms of what's required for VAT.

Broadly speaking, HM Customs and Excise define a business as being someone who is supplying goods and services in return for payment, although payment need not be in money. Your business activity must have a degree of frequency and scale over a continued period.

In other words if you're selling the occasional item here and there then you don't qualify for registration. Obviously this is to stop private individuals declaring themselves as businesses so as to take advantage of claiming back the VAT on their purchases.

When deciding whether or not to register for VAT try to look at the wider picture.

Case study: cycle hire
Let's imagine that you're planning to run a cycle hire business.

Your total hire stock is made up of 10 new bicycles which you have just purchased at £470 each including VAT at 17.5%, which equates to £70 VAT on each cycle.

Therefore the total amount of VAT that you have paid on your stock is £70 × 10 = £700. If your business is registered for VAT you can now re-claim this £700 as input tax.

But you must also charge VAT on your rentals, if you intend to rent these cycles out at £20 per day then you will have to add 17.5% VAT on top of this, which means you daily hire rate is now £23.50. You then will have to pay HM Customs and Excise £3.50 on each daily hire you make.

You decide that you will be sticking with your original bikes for a period of three years after which time you will then replace them with new bikes.

What this means is that although you have recouped £700 input tax having bought your cycles, you will now have to work out how much you will have to pay in VAT to HMCE over the three years you intend to keep the bikes.

You will also have to work out what other business costs you will incur over the next few years.

Cost could include:

- advertising
- cycle accessories
- staff uniforms
- maintenance of any business property

- stationery
- website costs.

The advantage of being registered for VAT means you can recoup the VAT element from all your business purchases where you have had to pay VAT.

Even one small advertisement in a glossy magazine can cost £200 per month plus VAT = £235. Thus over the three-year period you could claim up to £1,260 (36 months' VAT at £35 per month) on your advertising bill alone.

You may also find that you have to have your business premises painted once in the three years and provided you choose a VAT registered contractor you can claim back the VAT element.

As you can see the decision to register for VAT is something that only you can work out for your business. You need to work out your likely costs versus your sales income and see which is best.

If in doubt, my advice is not to register immediately but see how your business goes and then register later.

There are instances where you get back the VAT on certain items even though you have been trading for a period of time and not charging VAT.

Remember though if you supply only goods that are exempt from VAT you cannot claim back VAT on goods you purchase.

VAT exempt goods are different from zero rated goods.

Voluntary registration

If you decide to register for VAT when your turnover is less than the allowed limit you are doing what is known as voluntary registration.

By registering you will have to complete regular VAT returns which can be time consuming. A new flat rate system has been introduced to ease the burden of reporting for small businesses and this system is well worth taking a look at.

Where to go to get further information on VAT

It's beyond the scope of what we can include in this book to write a definitive guide to VAT. You can download all the information from the Customs and Excise website, which is located at http://www.hmce.gov.uk. Alternatively you can telephone them on 0845 010 9000.

They also run a number of business advice open days, which are free to attend and are run at various times throughout the year. These open days are run together with other agencies such as Inland Revenue, Health and Safety, Office of Fair Trading and others. Details can be found on their website http://www.businessadviceday.co.uk.

Index